Reading
Connections 5
From Academic Success to Everyday Fluency

Andrew E. Bennett

HEINLE
CENGAGE Learning™

Australia • Brazil • Japan • Korea • Mexico • Singapore • Spain • United Kingdom • United States

HEINLE
CENGAGE Learning

Reading Connections 5:
From Academic Success to Everyday Fluency

Andrew E. Bennett

Publisher, the Americas, Global, and Dictionaries:
Sherrise Roehr
Acquisitions Editor: Tom Jefferies
Senior Development Editor: Yeny Kim
Director of US Marketing: Jim McDonough
Senior Product Marketing Manager: Katie Kelley
Academic Marketing Manager: Caitlin Driscoll
Director of Global Marketing: Ian Martin
Director of Content and Media Production:
Michael Burggren
Senior Content Product Manager:
Maryellen E. Killeen
Senior Print Buyer: Mary Beth Hennebury

Images: All images: (c) istockphoto.com

For product information and technology assistance, contact us at
Cengage Learning Customer & Sales Support, 1-800-354-9706

For permission to use material from this text or product,
submit all requests online at **www.cengage.com/permissions**
Further permissions questions can be emailed to
permissionrequest@cengage.com

ISBN-13: 978-1-111-34863-2
ISBN-10: 1-111-34863-4

Heinle
20 Channel Center Street
Boston, MA 02210
USA

Cengage Learning is a leading provider of customized learning solutions with office locations around the globe, including Singapore, the United Kingdom, Australia, Mexico, Brazil and Japan. Locate your local office at
international.cengage.com/region

Cengage Learning products are represented in Canada by Nelson Education, Ltd.

Visit Heinle online at **elt.heinle.com**
Visit our corporate website at **www.cengage.com**

Printed in Canada
1 2 3 4 5 6 7 14 13 12 11 10

Contents

Introduction

Reading Connections is a NEW five-level series designed to develop the language and fluency necessary for success in real world and academic settings.

Reading Connections 5 contains 16 units centering on interesting articles about modern topics. A variety of important themes are covered, including the environment, health, technology, and more. Units open with a series of pre-reading exercises, followed by the main reading passage and a variety of skill building exercises. Each unit concludes with a supplementary reading passage.

Audio recordings of all student book readings are available in MP3 files on audio CD. The files are available for FREE online at elt.heinle.com/readingconnections

Also available is an assessment CD-ROM with Exam*View*®, which allows teachers to create tests and quizzes quickly and easily!

The following pages highlight and explain key features of the *Reading Connections* program.

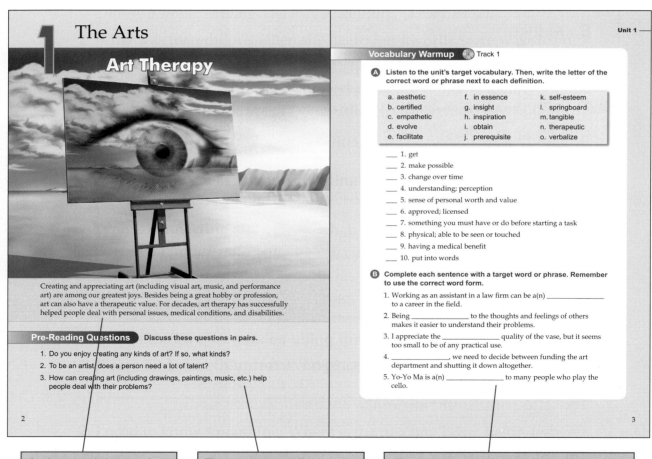

A short article preview opens the unit and helps the class prepare for the lesson.

Three pre-reading questions give students a chance to start thinking about the topic.

On the vocabulary warmup page, the unit's 15 target vocabulary items are listed. (They're also recorded on the audio CD.) Next, two sets of exercises check students' understanding of the target items.

Each reading passage is 600 words long. The unit's 15 target vocabulary items are in bold.

The reading passage is recorded on the audio CD.

Line numbers to the left of the reading passage provide an easy reference.

Part 1: Reading and Vocabulary Building

Reading Passage Track 2

Art has been a part of human cultures for millennia. Long before the development of writing systems, people painted on cave walls, carved statues, and made decorative bowls. Besides its **aesthetic** appeal, art also provides an opportunity for self-expression and understanding. As such,
5 drawings, dances, and dramas can be used for **therapeutic** purposes, acting as visual means to communicate thoughts and feelings. Driven by a patient's own creativity, art therapy can be a powerful part of the healing process.

Art therapy has existed as a formal type of psychotherapy since the 1940s. The practice involves using art as a tool to help patients understand
10 their feelings, express themselves, and gain **self-esteem**. Many types of visual art can be used, from painting to sculpture to performance arts like music, dance, and even puppetry. To participate, neither artistic talent nor experience in the medium are **prerequisites**.

Working with the patient is a **certified** art
15 therapist. He or she must have a strong educational background, including, typically, an undergraduate degree in art and a master's degree in art therapy. To
obtain the MA, coursework in subjects
20 like psychology and human development is required, in addition to 700-750 hours of practical experience in the field. After graduating and obtaining board certification, the therapist may work in a variety of settings, such as a hospital, nursing home, prison, school, or clinic.

In art therapy, the patient decides the symbolic meaning of his or her work.

25 In addition to being honest and **empathetic**, the therapist must create a safe and supportive environment, forming a bond of trust with the patient. Doing so is essential, as the patient may have experienced severe abuse, trauma, or

---

¹ millennium (plural: millennia) – period of one thousand years
⁸ psychotherapy – medical practice involving the treatment of mental problems
¹³ medium – art form or material (such as clay, metal, etc.)
²⁷ trauma – emotionally or physically painful experience

4

Unit 1

illness. In individual and group sessions, patients talk about their work. For example, a series of drawings may contain illustrations of an angry dog, a
30 symbolic image which someone with PTSD (post traumatic stress disorder) might associate with an accident. Importantly, it is the patient who provides the explanation of these images, not the therapist.

A number of conditions can be treated with art therapy. Patients dealing with depression can develop higher self-esteem and improved social
35 relationships. Those dealing with addiction can **facilitate** change through, in part, a recognition of their addiction. And, people with autism can improve their imagination, hand-eye coordination, and communication skills, to name a few of the benefits. Art therapy is especially helpful for patients who have trouble **verbalizing** their feelings and for those who have
40 been unsuccessful with traditional "talk therapy." **In essence**, the artwork provides a **springboard** for communication.

The visual record that's created may be kept in an art journal, so changes can be tracked over time. Because they are **tangible**, these pictures, sculptures, and designs can have an empowering effect. For instance, a sufferer of
45 anorexia may have trouble talking about sadness or pain, yet once the feelings are given form, they can be looked at, identified, and discussed. As the patient draws, sculpts, or dances, he or she literally has control over the work, which can be a starting point for improving a sense of self-worth.

Over time, the body of work may **evolve**, reflecting a growing degree of
50 personal **insight**. Eventually, if a patient wishes, his or her art can even be publicly displayed, providing hope and **inspiration** to others. At the University of California, Irvine, a special exhibit called "Memories in the Making" showed the paintings of several people with Alzheimer's disease. Though the sufferers of the disease may have had trouble communicating
55 with words, they were, through brush strokes and colors, able to reach out and make connections with the community.

---

³⁵ addiction – being dependent on a drug (such as alcohol)
³⁶ autism – a developmental condition making it hard to form relationships, develop language skills, etc.
⁴⁵ anorexia – a mental illness leading to a severe loss of appetite
⁵³ Alzheimer's – a disease affecting memory (common amongst older people)

5

Beneath the reading passage is a simplified glossary. To the left of each glossary item is the line number where it can be found.

A caption beneath each image shows its relevance to the article.

Following the passage are five reading comprehension questions including main idea, detail, vocabulary, and analysis questions.

These vocabulary exercises check students' knowledge of the unit's 15 target vocabulary items. There are three types of exercises: synonym, fill in the blank, and word form.

Reading Comprehension Choose the best answer.

.... Main Idea

1. ( ) What is the main idea?
   A. Art therapy has been used for more than half a century.
   B. Art therapy can only treat a narrow range of conditions.
   C. Art therapy provides a visual platform for treating problems.
   D. Art therapy is an excellent treatment for autistic people.

.... Detail

2. ( ) Who interprets the symbols in a patient's work?
   A. The therapist   B. The patient himself or herself
   C. Other patients in group sessions   D. Family members

.... Vocabulary

3. ( ) In line 27, what does "essential" mean?
   A. necessary   B. creative
   C. understanding   D. therapeutic

.... Analysis

4. ( ) What does the article imply about art therapists?
   A. They should tell patients about any abuse they've experienced.
   B. They are usually famous artists or art critics.
   C. They need to be well educated and highly trained.
   D. They receive board certification before obtaining their MA.

5. ( ) In what way is an art journal empowering for a patient?
   A. Its contents are directed by the art therapist.
   B. Journals are always shown to people in the community.
   C. The patient controls the types of images he or she creates.
   D. It makes patients unaware of their problems.

Short Answers Answer each question based on the article.

1. What are three types of performance art that can be used for art therapy?
   _____

2. To obtain an MA, how many hours of practical experience does a therapist need?
   _____

3. How can art therapy help someone with an addiction?
   _____

Vocabulary Building

A Choose the answer that means the same as the word or phrase in italics.

1. Manuela says her interests have *evolved*, so these days she does more pottery than painting.
   A. created   B. changed   C. identified

2. *In essence*, our challenge is to redesign the car so it's half as heavy and twice as fast.
   A. Faithfully   B. Casually   C. Basically

3. The pool needs a lifeguard, but you have to be *certified* for the position.
   A. licensed   B. experienced   C. motivated

4. Complimenting a person can help him or her build *self-esteem*.
   A. self-worth   B. self-doubt   C. self-control

5. City residents appreciate *tangible* improvements like new sidewalks and upgraded street lights.
   A. costly   B. promised   C. physical

B Complete each sentence with the best word. Remember to use the correct word form.

| therapeutic | prerequisite | verbalize | springboard | insight |

1. Speaking Spanish isn't a(n) _____ for working at the trading company, but it is a big help.

2. Peter's analysis showed a deep _____ into the painting.

3. Some feelings which are hard to _____ may be expressed through art.

4. After a hard day at work, a relaxing evening can be very _____.

5. An internship or part-time job makes a great _____ to a career in the film industry.

C Circle the correct form of each word.

1. (Obtain/Obtaining) everyone's approval for the proposal will not be easy.

2. It's important for children to learn to feel (empathy/empathize) towards others.

3. Many people are (inspiration/inspired) when they visit the Grand Canyon.

4. Mr. Torez will help (facilitating/facilitate) your transfer to the new branch.

5. There's no question the chair is (aesthetic/aesthetically) beautiful, but how comfortable is it?

6

7

These three questions are also based on the reading passage. Answers should be one sentence long.

Improving knowledge of word parts is an excellent way to strengthen reading skills. In this section, three word parts (one prefix, one root, and one suffix) are presented. They're based on word parts found in the reading passage. A short exercise checks students' knowledge of the material.

Three discussion questions give students a chance to talk about the topic. Some questions are based on the reading passage. Others, which are more general, are based on the unit's larger theme.

Part 2: Focus Areas

Focus on Language

Word Parts

Study the word parts in the chart. Then, read the following pairs of sentences. Circle if the second sentence is true or false.

Word Part	Meaning	Examples
ob-	against	obscene, obtuse
-psych(o)-	mind	psychotic, psychology
-er	performer of an action	farmer, explorer

1. Ms. Marriot, the lawyer for the defense, objected to the question.
   Ms. Marriot did not approve of the question. (True / False)
2. The young man's psychosis caused him to see things that weren't there.
   His situation was caused by a mental disorder. (True / False)
3. Michael's dream as a child was to become a circus performer.
   When he was young, he had no interest in working in the circus. (True / False)

Grammar   Modal + Passive Voice

Using the passive voice with a modal allows for the construction of many useful sentence types. We can use the structure to describe an action that someone should, could, may, or might do.

Structure: s + should / might / could / etc. + be + pp

Ex: All packages should be delivered to the mail room.

Ex: The air quality could be improved by people driving less.

Complete each sentence using the passive. Use the verb in parentheses.

1. Joe might _____ (punish) for being late so often.
2. The application form must _____ (fill out) in black ink.
3. Should people with pets _____ (allow) into stores?
4. The prices may _____ (reduce) later this month.
5. The furniture could _____ (make) more cheaply in Mexico.

8

Focus on Production   Unit 1

Talk About It   Discuss these questions in small groups.

1. If you were to undergo art therapy, what type of art would you use?
2. In your opinion, what problems or conditions can benefit the most from art therapy?
3. Art therapy is sometimes considered an "alternative" therapy (in other words, not involving medicine or surgery). What other alternative therapies are you familiar with?

Write About It

Question: Should medical insurance plans be required to cover art therapy? Give two reasons to support your opinion. Prepare by writing notes on the lines below. The first few words of the paragraph are written to help you get started.

Opinion: _____

Reason 1: _____

Reason 2: _____

If all medical insurance covered art therapy, that would _____

_____

_____

_____

_____

_____

_____

_____

_____

9

This section presents practical grammar structures with the goal of improving communicative grammar skills. First, a short, simple explanation is given. That's followed by structural models (if applicable) and example sentences. Finally, a short exercise checks students' ability to apply what they've learned.

In this guided exercise, students write a paragraph about the topic. Several lines are provided so students can create a mini-outline. The first few words of the paragraph are also given. Paragraphs should be short (less than 10 sentences long). Though there is no single "correct" answer, a model paragraph is provided in the answer key on the website.

From unit to unit, this section alternates between a short conversation and a short listening passage. Every conversation and listening passage includes three of the unit's target vocabulary items, for recycling purposes.

The audio script can be found on the website.

The final page of each unit contains a supplementary reading passage. This 250-word article provides a deeper insight into certain aspects of the unit's topic.

The conversations and short listening passages are recorded on the audio CD.

The article is recorded on the audio CD.

Focus on Testing

Listening Listen to the conversation. Then, answer the following questions.

 Track 3

1. (   ) Where are the people?
   (A) At a magazine company   (B) At a design school
   (C) At an art gallery   (D) At a friend's house

2. (   ) What does the man suggest about Harrington's work?
   (A) It has changed over the last decade.
   (B) It isn't very inspiring.
   (C) It is similar to that of other artists.
   (D) It looks like ad work.

3. (   ) What would the woman like to see Harrington do?
   (A) Take the man's advice   (B) Paint in darker colors
   (C) Develop a personal style   (D) Use classical techniques

Reading Read the letter. Then, answer the following questions.

Dear Ms. Philips,

Thank you for your e-mail regarding internship opportunities at Silverton Academy. There is an opening next semester, which starts in three weeks. The only prerequisite is an art background, which I see you have as you're a junior in art college. Also, since we work with special needs children, all staff must be very patient and empathetic.

If the timeframe works for you, the next step would be an interview, which I could fit in next Wednesday afternoon. Before then, please send me a short letter introducing yourself (not a résumé, as I have that). We'd especially like an insight into your philosophy about art and how it relates to working with children.

Adrian Diaz

1. (   ) What is the purpose of this e-mail?
   (A) To respond to an inquiry   (B) To offer a position
   (C) To announce a policy   (D) To reject an application

2. (   ) The word "timeframe" in paragraph 2, line 1, is closest in meaning to
   (A) semester   (B) timeliness
   (C) scheduling   (D) internship

3. (   ) What does Mr. Diaz want Ms. Philips to send him?
   (A) A written introduction   (B) A detailed résumé
   (C) A letter of recommendation   (D) A short proposal

Supplementary Reading - *The Therapist's Role*   Track 4

Art therapy involves the interaction of three elements: the patient, his or her artwork, and the art therapist. The therapist's role is to facilitate a patient's understanding of his or her sculptures, drawings, or dances, both in discrete terms (each individual piece) and longitudinal terms (the collected body of work over time). To accomplish this task, the therapist must earn a patient's trust, both by exhibiting concern and by listening carefully to the patient's thoughts about his or her artwork, ideas, and feelings.

Therapists need to be skilled at detecting patterns across several works of art. For instance, some patients may draw the same items (such as a wolf or barn) over and over. This so-called "stereotyped art" provides sufferers of abuse, trauma, or mental disorders with a sense of security and control. Yet depending on  the context, the items may differ in meaning. The therapist needs to pay careful attention to the usage and frequency of such images. Eventually, through many group and individual sessions, patients may develop a better understanding of their personal symbols.

The art therapist also needs to be familiar with the application of a variety of art forms. That way, the patient can be provided with as wide a range of choices as possible. What's more, during the course of treatment, the therapist may actually become a participant, creating art alongside the patient. Doing so helps build a bond of trust, showing the patient that the therapist, rather than just an impersonal observer, is directly involved in the healing process.

Read each sentence. Circle if it is true (T) or false (F).

1. For a therapist, being a good listener is an important part of earning a patient's trust.   T / F
2. Stereotyped images carry the same meaning in every work of art.   T / F
3. It takes time for patients to understand frequently drawn images.   T / F
4. Art therapists always specialize in one type of art.   T / F
5. Art therapists may draw or sculpt during a session with a patient.   T / F

From unit to unit, this section alternates between a short reading passage (such as an article, e-mail, report, etc.) and a cloze passage. Every reading passage recycles three of the unit's target vocabulary items.

Five true and false questions check students' comprehension.

Scope and Sequence

	Theme	Reading Skills	Word Parts	Grammar	Test Preparation
1	The Arts	Identifying the main idea and details; using vocabulary in context; recognizing implications	**prefix:** ob- **root:** -psych(o)- **suffix:** -er	Modal + Passive Voice	**Listening:** Conversation about art **Reading:** Letter about an internship
2	Science and Technology	Identifying the main idea and details; using vocabulary in context; recognizing implications	**prefix:** un- **root:** -vis- **suffix:** -graphy	Preposition + Adjective Clause	**Listening:** Announcement of a breakthrough **Reading:** Cloze passage article
3	Business	Identifying the main idea and details; using vocabulary in context	**prefix:** prim- **root:** -cogn- **suffix:** -back	Whereas vs. Whereby	**Listening:** Conversation about a job **Reading:** Article about a company
4	The Environment	Identifying the main idea and details; using vocabulary in context; making inferences	**prefix:** agr(i)- **root:** -port- **suffix:** -ity	What better way...than by	**Listening:** Speech about a charity **Reading:** Cloze passage article
5	The Internet	Identifying the main idea and details; using vocabulary in context; recognizing implications	**prefix:** sur- **root:** -cept- **suffix:** -ship	What's... may be	**Listening:** Conversation about a party **Reading:** Announcement for a website
6	Growing and Aging	Identifying the main idea and details; using vocabulary in context	**prefix:** neg- **root:** -cent- **suffix:** -ism	Passive Form of the Present Progressive	**Listening:** Answering machine message **Reading:** Cloze passage article

	Theme	Reading Skills	Word Parts	Grammar	Test Preparation
7	Nature	Identifying the main idea and details; using vocabulary in context; recognizing suggestions	**prefix:** op- **root:** -techn(o)- **suffix:** -cide	Likewise vs. Likely	**Listening:** Conversation about a garden **Reading:** Conference information
8	Entertainment	Identifying the main idea and details; using vocabulary in context; making inferences	**prefix:** super- **root:** -nat- **suffix:** -ary	Appositives	**Listening:** Business news report **Reading:** Cloze passage article
9	Space	Identifying the main idea and details; using vocabulary in context; recognizing sequences	**prefix:** micro- **root:** -photo- **suffix:** -some	The more... the more	**Listening:** Conversation about a design **Reading:** Article about space
10	Culture	Identifying the main idea and details; using vocabulary in context	**prefix:** intro/intra- **root:** -dem(o)- **suffix:** -ous	To do so & In doing so	**Listening:** Radio program preview **Reading:** Cloze passage article
11	Health	Identifying the main idea and details; using vocabulary in context; recognizing implications	**prefix:** sub- **root:** -cis- **suffix:** -ence	Reflexive Pronouns	**Listening:** Conversation about an accident **Reading:** Advertisement for a gym
12	Law and Crime	Identifying the main idea and details; using vocabulary in context; recognizing implications	**prefix:** out- **root:** -mar- **suffix:** -age	Conditional sentences with "should"	**Listening:** Announcement of a retirement **Reading:** Cloze passage article

	Theme	Reading Skills	Word Parts	Grammar	Test Preparation
13	Identity	Identifying the main idea and details; using vocabulary in context; recognizing suggestions	**prefix:** cor- **root:** -mit- **suffix:** -wide	Present Perfect + Passive + Phrasal Verbs	**Listening:** Conversation about a trip **Reading:** Memo about a safety issue
14	Social Issues	Identifying the main idea and details; using vocabulary in context; making inferences	**prefix:** de- **root:** -dom- **suffix:** -ible	Expressions of Quantity + Subject/Verb Agreement	**Listening:** Report about an earthquake **Reading:** Cloze passage article
15	Globalization	Identifying the main idea and details; using vocabulary in context; recognizing implications	**prefix:** over- **root:** -sen(s)- **suffix:** -or	It's not a question of...	**Listening:** Conversation about currencies **Reading:** Letter of response
16	The Future	Identifying the main idea and details; using vocabulary in context	**prefix:** multi- **root:** -gen- **suffix:** -ist	By + future vs. By + future perfect	**Listening:** Speech from a tour guide **Reading:** Cloze passage article

1 The Arts

Art Therapy

Creating and appreciating art (including visual art, music, and performance art) are among our greatest joys. Besides being a great hobby or profession, art can also have a therapeutic value. For decades, art therapy has successfully helped people deal with personal issues, medical conditions, and disabilities.

Pre-Reading Questions   Discuss these questions in pairs.

1. Do you enjoy creating any kinds of art? If so, what kinds?

2. To be an artist, does a person need a lot of talent?

3. How can creating art (including drawings, paintings, music, etc.) help people deal with their problems?

Vocabulary Warmup Track 1

A Listen to the unit's target vocabulary. Then, write the letter of the correct word or phrase next to each definition.

a. aesthetic	f. in essence	k. self-esteem
b. certified	g. insight	l. springboard
c. empathetic	h. inspiration	m. tangible
d. evolve	i. obtain	n. therapeutic
e. facilitate	j. prerequisite	o. verbalize

____ 1. get

____ 2. make possible

____ 3. change over time

____ 4. understanding; perception

____ 5. sense of personal worth and value

____ 6. approved; licensed

____ 7. something you must have or do before starting a task

____ 8. physical; able to be seen or touched

____ 9. having a medical benefit

____ 10. put into words

B Complete each sentence with a target word or phrase. Remember to use the correct word form.

1. Working as an assistant in a law firm can be a(n) _____ to a career in the field.

2. Being _____ to the thoughts and feelings of others makes it easier to understand their problems.

3. I appreciate the _____ quality of the vase, but it seems too small to be of any practical use.

4. _____, we need to decide between funding the art department and shutting it down altogether.

5. Yo-Yo Ma is a(n) _____ to many people who play the cello.

Part 1: Reading and Vocabulary Building

1   Art has been a part of human cultures for millennia. Long before the
development of writing systems, people painted on cave walls, carved
statues, and made decorative bowls. Besides its **aesthetic** appeal, art also
provides an opportunity for self-expression and understanding. As such,
5   drawings, dances, and dramas can be used for **therapeutic** purposes, acting
as visual means to communicate thoughts and feelings. Driven by a patient's
own creativity, art therapy can be a powerful part of the healing process.

Art therapy has existed as a formal type of psychotherapy since the 1940s.
The practice involves using art as a tool to help patients understand
10   their feelings, express themselves, and gain **self-esteem**. Many types of
visual art can be used, from painting to sculpture to performance arts like
music, dance, and even puppetry. To participate, neither artistic talent nor
experience in the medium are **prerequisites**.

Working with the patient is a **certified** art
15   therapist. He or she must have a strong
educational background, including,
typically, an undergraduate degree in art
and a master's degree in art therapy. To
obtain the MA, coursework in subjects
20   like psychology and human development
is required, in addition to 700-750 hours
of practical experience in the field. After

*In art therapy, the patient decides the
symbolic meaning of his or her work.*

graduating and obtaining board certification, the therapist may work in a
variety of settings, such as a hospital, nursing home, prison, school, or clinic.

25   In addition to being honest and **empathetic**, the therapist must create a safe
and supportive environment, forming a bond of trust with the patient. Doing
so is essential, as the patient may have experienced severe abuse, trauma, or

---

¹ millennium (plural: millennia) – period of one thousand years
⁸ psychotherapy – medical practice involving the treatment of mental problems
¹³ medium – art form or material (such as clay, metal, etc.)
²⁷ trauma – emotionally or physically painful experience

illness. In individual and group sessions, patients talk about their work. For example, a series of drawings may contain illustrations of an angry dog, a
30 symbolic image which someone with PTSD (post traumatic stress disorder) might associate with an accident. Importantly, it is the patient who provides the explanation of these images, not the therapist.

A number of conditions can be treated with art therapy. Patients dealing with depression can develop higher self-esteem and improved social
35 relationships. Those dealing with addiction can **facilitate** change through, in part, a recognition of their addiction. And, people with autism can improve their imagination, hand-eye coordination, and communication skills, to name a few of the benefits. Art therapy is especially helpful for patients who have trouble **verbalizing** their feelings and for those who have
40 been unsuccessful with traditional "talk therapy." **In essence**, the artwork provides a **springboard** for communication.

The visual record that's created may be kept in an art journal, so changes can be tracked over time. Because they are **tangible**, these pictures, sculptures, and designs can have an empowering effect. For instance, a sufferer of
45 anorexia may have trouble talking about sadness or pain, yet once the feelings are given form, they can be looked at, identified, and discussed. As the patient draws, sculpts, or dances, he or she literally has control over the work, which can be a starting point for improving a sense of self-worth.

Over time, the body of work may **evolve**, reflecting a growing degree of
50 personal **insight**. Eventually, if a patient wishes, his or her art can even be publicly displayed, providing hope and **inspiration** to others. At the University of California, Irvine, a special exhibit called "Memories in the Making" showed the paintings of several people with Alzheimer's disease. Though the sufferers of the disease may have had trouble communicating
55 with words, they were, through brush strokes and colors, able to reach out and make connections with the community.

---

[35] addiction – being dependent on a drug (such as alcohol)
[36] autism – a developmental condition making it hard to form relationships, develop language skills, etc.
[45] anorexia – a mental illness leading to a severe loss of appetite
[53] Alzheimer's – a disease affecting memory (common amongst older people)

Choose the best answer.

.... **Main Idea**

1. (   ) What is the main idea?
   A. Art therapy has been used for more than half a century.
   B. Art therapy can only treat a narrow range of conditions.
   C. Art therapy provides a visual platform for treating problems.
   D. Art therapy is an excellent treatment for autistic people.

.... **Detail**

2. (   ) Who interprets the symbols in a patient's work?
   A. The therapist   B. The patient himself or herself
   C. Other patients in group sessions   D. Family members

.... **Vocabulary**

3. (   ) In line 27, what does "essential" mean?
   A. necessary   B. creative
   C. understanding   D. therapeutic

.... **Analysis**

4. (   ) What does the article imply about art therapists?
   A. They should tell patients about any abuse they've experienced.
   B. They are usually famous artists or art critics.
   C. They need to be well educated and highly trained.
   D. They receive board certification before obtaining their MA.

5. (   ) In what way is an art journal empowering for a patient?
   A. Its contents are directed by the art therapist.
   B. Journals are always shown to people in the community.
   C. The patient controls the types of images he or she creates.
   D. It makes patients unaware of their problems.

Short Answers   **Answer each question based on the article.**

1. What are three types of performance art that can be used for art therapy?

   _____

2. To obtain an MA, how many hours of practical experience does a therapist need?

   _____

3. How can art therapy help someone with an addiction?

   _____

Vocabulary Building

A **Choose the answer that means the same as the word or phrase in italics.**

1. Manuela says her interests have *evolved*, so these days she does more pottery than painting.
   A. created   B. changed   C. identified

2. *In essence*, our challenge is to redesign the car so it's half as heavy and twice as fast.
   A. Faithfully   B. Casually   C. Basically

3. The pool needs a lifeguard, but you have to be *certified* for the position.
   A. licensed   B. experienced   C. motivated

4. Complimenting a person can help him or her build *self-esteem*.
   A. self-worth   B. self-doubt   C. self-control

5. City residents appreciate *tangible* improvements like new sidewalks and upgraded street lights.
   A. costly   B. promised   C. physical

B **Complete each sentence with the best word. Remember to use the correct word form.**

therapeutic	prerequisite	verbalize	springboard	insight

1. Speaking Spanish isn't a(n) _____ for working at the trading company, but it is a big help.

2. Peter's analysis showed a deep _____ into the painting.

3. Some feelings which are hard to _____ may be expressed through art.

4. After a hard day at work, a relaxing evening can be very _____.

5. An internship or part-time job makes a great _____ to a career in the film industry.

C **Circle the correct form of each word.**

1. (Obtain/Obtaining) everyone's approval for the proposal will not be easy.

2. It's important for children to learn to feel (empathy/empathize) towards others.

3. Many people are (inspiration/inspired) when they visit the Grand Canyon.

4. Mr. Torez will help (facilitating/facilitate) your transfer to the new branch.

5. There's no question the chair is (aesthetic/aesthetically) beautiful, but how comfortable is it?

Part 2: Focus Areas

Focus on Language

Word Parts

Study the word parts in the chart. Then, read the following pairs of sentences. Circle if the second sentence is true or false.

Word Part	Meaning	Examples
ob-	against	obscene, obtuse
-psych(o)-	mind	psychotic, psychology
-er	performer of an action	farmer, explorer

1. Ms. Marriot, the lawyer for the defense, objected to the question.
   Ms. Marriot did not approve of the question. (True / False)

2. The young man's psychosis caused him to see things that weren't there.
   His situation was caused by a mental disorder. (True / False)

3. Michael's dream as a child was to become a circus performer.
   When he was young, he had no interest in working in the circus. (True / False)

Grammar *Modal + Passive Voice*

Using the passive voice with a modal allows for the construction of many useful sentence types. We can use the structure to describe an action that someone should, could, may, or might do.

Structure: **s + should / might / could / etc. + be + pp**

Ex: All packages should be delivered to the mail room.

Ex: The air quality could be improved by people driving less.

Complete each sentence using the passive. Use the verb in parentheses.

1. Joe might _____ (punish) for being late so often.

2. The application form must _____ (fill out) in black ink.

3. Should people with pets _____ (allow) into stores?

4. The prices may _____ (reduce) later this month.

5. The furniture could _____ (make) more cheaply in Mexico.

Talk About It   Discuss these questions in small groups.

1. If you were to undergo art therapy, what type of art would you use?

2. In your opinion, what problems or conditions can benefit the most from art therapy?

3. Art therapy is sometimes considered an "alternative" therapy (in other words, not involving medicine or surgery). What other alternative therapies are you familiar with?

Write About It

Question: Should medical insurance plans be required to cover art therapy? Give two reasons to support your opinion. Prepare by writing notes on the lines below. The first few words of the paragraph are written to help you get started.

Opinion: _____

Reason 1: _____

Reason 2: _____

If all medical insurance covered art therapy, that would _____

_____

_____

_____

_____

_____

_____

_____

Listening   Listen to the conversation. Then, answer the following questions.

Track 3   1. (   ) Where are the people?
        (A) At a magazine company   (B) At a design school
        (C) At an art gallery   (D) At a friend's house

    2. (   ) What does the man suggest about Harrington's work?
        (A) It has changed over the last decade.
        (B) It isn't very inspiring.
        (C) It is similar to that of other artists.
        (D) It looks like ad work.

    3. (   ) What would the woman like to see Harrington do?
        (A) Take the man's advice   (B) Paint in darker colors
        (C) Develop a personal style   (D) Use classical techniques

Reading   Read the letter. Then, answer the following questions.

Dear Ms. Philips,

Thank you for your e-mail regarding internship opportunities at Silverton Academy. There is an opening next semester, which starts in three weeks. The only prerequisite is an art background, which I see you have as you're a junior in art college. Also, since we work with special needs children, all staff must be very patient and empathetic.

If the timeframe works for you, the next step would be an interview, which I could fit in next Wednesday afternoon. Before then, please send me a short letter introducing yourself (not a résumé, as I have that). We'd especially like an insight into your philosophy about art and how it relates to working with children.

Adrian Diaz

1. (   ) What is the purpose of this e-mail?
    (A) To respond to an inquiry   (B) To offer a position
    (C) To announce a policy   (D) To reject an application

2. (   ) The word "timeframe" in paragraph 2, line 1, is closest in meaning to
    (A) semester   (B) timeliness
    (C) scheduling   (D) internship

3. (   ) What does Mr. Diaz want Ms. Philips to send him?
    (A) A written introduction   (B) A detailed résumé
    (C) A letter of recommendation   (D) A short proposal

Supplementary Reading - *The Therapist's Role* Track 4

Art therapy involves the interaction of three elements: the patient, his or her artwork, and the art therapist. The therapist's role is to facilitate a patient's understanding of his or her sculptures, drawings, or dances, both in discrete terms (each individual piece) and longitudinal terms (the collected body of work over time). To accomplish this task, the therapist must earn a patient's trust, both by exhibiting concern and by listening carefully to the patient's thoughts about his or her artwork, ideas, and feelings.

Therapists need to be skilled at detecting patterns across several works of art. For instance, some patients may draw the same items (such as a wolf or barn) over and over. This so-called "stereotyped art" provides sufferers of abuse, trauma, or mental disorders with a sense of security and control. Yet depending on  the context, the items may differ in meaning. The therapist needs to pay careful attention to the usage and frequency of such images. Eventually, through many group and individual sessions, patients may develop a better understanding of their personal symbols.

The art therapist also needs to be familiar with the application of a variety of art forms. That way, the patient can be provided with as wide a range of choices as possible. What's more, during the course of treatment, the therapist may actually become a participant, creating art alongside the patient. Doing so helps build a bond of trust, showing the patient that the therapist, rather than just an impersonal observer, is directly involved in the healing process.

Read each sentence. Circle if it is true (T) or false (F).

1. For a therapist, being a good listener is an important part of earning a patient's trust.   T / F

2. Stereotyped images carry the same meaning in every work of art.   T / F

3. It takes time for patients to understand frequently drawn images.   T / F

4. Art therapists always specialize in one type of art.   T / F

5. Art therapists may draw or sculpt during a session with a patient.   T / F

Science and Technology

2

From Science Fiction to Reality

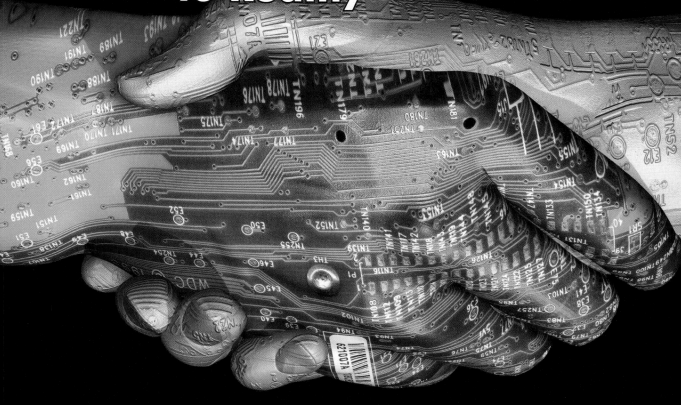

Science fiction has been a popular genre for more than a century. We love fantastic tales of space explorers and underwater civilizations. These stories have also inspired many real-world scientists. Through research and hard work, they've turned some incredible ideas into amazing inventions.

Pre-Reading Questions   Discuss these questions in pairs.

1. What kinds of stories do you enjoy? (ex: action, romance, science fiction)

2. Can you think of any items that appeared in stories or movies before being made into actual products?

3. How about in the future? What fictitious products might eventually become reality?

Vocabulary Warmup Track 5

A Listen to the unit's target vocabulary. Then, write the letter of the correct word or phrase next to each definition.

a. ample	f. hostile	k. precedent
b. brainstorm	g. inject	l. profoundly
c. dedication	h. microscopic	m. replicate
d. encounter	i. nexus	n. teleportation
e. equipped with	j. outsmart	o. thermal

____ 1. make an exact copy

____ 2. deeply

____ 3. connection; point of intersection

____ 4. fierce; unfriendly

____ 5. plenty; more than enough

____ 6. come up with new ideas

____ 7. commitment

____ 8. extremely small

____ 9. related to heat

____ 10. come across; find

B Complete each sentence with a target word or phrase. Remember to use the correct word form.

1. I doubt you'll be able to _____ Gerard. He's a genius.

2. To help prove a case, lawyers often look for one or more legal _____ from earlier cases and judgments.

3. The vaccine is usually _____ into a patient's arm.

4. The car comes _____ a GPS system which you can use to get directions to any address.

5. If _____ becomes possible for people, it may mean the end of other forms of transportation like trains and airplanes.

Part 1: Reading and Vocabulary Building

1   We live in a time when robot vehicles roam across other planets, tiny
machines course through blood vessels, and unmanned aircraft fly over
hostile territory. Many of these ideas were envisioned long ago by science
fiction writers. Their work has inspired engineers and researchers who have
5   gone on to develop products similar to the ones they **encountered** in fictional
stories. In numerous fields, such as space exploration, robotics, military
hardware, and medical research, the visions of science fiction writers have
provided **ample** inspiration for new technologies.

There has long been a **nexus** between science fiction writing and hard
10   science. In fact, several of the top authors of the 20th century, like Isaac
Asimov and Arthur C. Clarke, were trained scientists. Back in 1945, a
meeting was held between researchers and authors like Robert Heinlein.
They met to map out long-term goals for scientific advancement. More
recently, NASA, the US space agency, has worked with authors to
15   **brainstorm** ideas for future missions. Likewise, the European Space Agency
has employed people to read classic works of science fiction in search of
promising ideas.

It's not surprising that space exploration has been **profoundly** impacted by
science fiction. In stories, TV shows, and movies, explorers are **equipped**
20   **with** laser guns and other wondrous gadgets. Some of them are now a
reality. For instance, NASA has created a system, called NUGGET, which
can detect signs of life from a distance. It's similar to the "tricorder" device
used in the classic 1960s TV show *Star Trek*. Also, NASA's Deep Space One
spacecraft, launched in 1998, used an ion propulsion engine, an idea also
25   featured decades earlier in *Star Trek*.

Robotics is another area where the once unreal is now taking shape. Artificial
intelligence is at the center of many efforts, as researchers seek to create

---

3   envision – think up; imagine
9   hard science – real-world science such as physics, chemistry, etc.
24 ion – an atom with an electrical charge
24 propulsion – the force which provides forward movement
26 take shape – happen; become reality

machines that can **outsmart** people. Scientists at the University of Reading, England, have already created a brain made from the neurons of rats. The
30 next step is to use human neurons to **replicate** a brain that can control a robot. In fact, back in 1965, Keith Laumer wrote *A Plague of Dreams*, in which aliens stole human brains to use in robot bodies.

The military is also interested in robots and other futuristic technologies for use on the battlefield. There is ample **precedent** for such ideas in
35 science fiction stories. In "Second Variety," a 1953 Philip K. Dick short story, intelligent robots fight with deadly efficiency. More than 50 years later, the US military has working systems like the Predator, an unmanned, remote-controlled
40 aircraft. There are also robotic vehicles which carry cameras and **thermal** imaging equipment. By entering a potentially dangerous area, they can determine if it's safe for human soldiers to enter.

Unmanned aircraft have leapt from the pages of fiction to reality.

45 Amazing technologies are also being developed to save lives. One of the most exciting areas is nanotechnology. In the 1966 sci-fi film *Fantastic Voyage*, a **microscopic** submarine journeyed through a person's body. Nanobots now have the potential to do just that. In Montreal, Canada, researchers have developed a way to **inject** a nanobot into a blood vessel. It's hoped that in
50 the near future, sophisticated mini-machines may travel through a patient's body, targeting infections and tumors.

As exciting as current realizations of science fiction are, the future looks even more incredible. Areas like virtual reality, holography, and even **teleportation** could make daily life seem like a scene from a fantasy story.
55 The imaginations of science fiction writers, and the **dedication** they inspire in the world's scientists, will certainly be key ingredients as we push forward into the future.

---

[29] neuron – nerve cell
[31] plague – terrible disease, pest, or series of problems
[46] nanotechnology – the science of manufacturing extremely small things
[50] sophisticated – highly advanced
[51] tumor – unnatural cell growth (often caused by cancer) in one's body
[53] holography – using lasers to create and show 3D images

Choose the best answer.

.... **Main Idea**

1. (   ) What is the main idea?
   A. Science fiction has influenced research and advances in many fields.
   B. Recent developments in robotics have been very exciting.
   C. Isaac Asimov was an influential writer as well as a trained scientist.
   D. Some famous science fiction writers were also scientists.

.... **Detail**

2. (   ) In what year did an author write about warrior robots?
   A. 1953
   B. 1965
   C. 1966
   D. 1998

.... **Vocabulary**

3. (   ) In line 42, what does "potentially" mean?
   A. possibly   B. unfortunately
   C. definitely   D. seemingly

.... **Analysis**

4. (   ) What type of science fiction work included nanotechnology before its invention?
   A. A movie   B. A novel
   C. A short story   D. A TV show

5. (   ) What does the article imply about the future?
   A. Short stories will be the most influential type of fictional writing.
   B. Scientists will rely less on the visions of authors and filmmakers.
   C. Teleportation and holography will be perfected within a few years.
   D. We'll see even more developments inspired by science fiction.

Short Answers **Answer each question based on the article.**

1. Why did a group of researchers and authors get together in 1945?

_____

2. Why did the European Space Agency hire people to read science fiction?

_____

3. What are two inventions which are similar to devices seen in *Star Trek*?

_____

Vocabulary Building

A **Choose the answer that means the same as the word or phrase in italics.**

1. Researchers use advanced equipment to design machines on a *microscopic* level.
   A. very small   B. very rare   C. very unusual

2. When the hikers *encountered* a bear, they froze like statues, too scared to move or call for help.
   A. chased   B. angered   C. met

3. There's *ample* wood to build a fence around the house.
   A. residential   B. premium   C. sufficient

4. *Thermal* shields protect spacecraft during re-entry into the atmosphere.
   A. Space   B. Heat   C. Flight

5. The car comes *equipped with* a DVD player and a large monitor.
   A. contrasted with   B. associated with   C. provided with

B **Complete each sentence with the best word. Remember to use the correct word form.**

> outsmart   precedent   brainstorm   nexus   teleportation

1. Once a month, we have _____ sessions to come up with new ideas for ice cream flavors.

2. The _____ of small particles is one thing, but sending large objects from one place to another is something else altogether.

3. Even the world's best chess players have trouble _____ the fastest supercomputers.

4. The _____ between reading and vocabulary development has been thoroughly researched.

5. There's no _____ for a robot adopting a child.

C **Circle the correct form of each word.**

1. The medicine can be administered by (inject/injection) or via a pill.

2. The suggestion to raise ticket prices met with a (hostile/hostility) reaction.

3. Stephen is so (dedicated/dedication) to his job that he cancelled his vacation to attend a company picnic.

4. We both have (profound/profoundly) respect for Mr. and Mrs. Lee.

5. (Replication/Replicating) last year's success will be hard, given the economic climate.

Focus on Language

Word Parts

Study the word parts in the chart. Then, read the following pairs of sentences. Circle if the second sentence is true or false.

Word Part	Meaning	Examples
un-	not	unplanned, unknown
-vis-	sight	visual, supervise
-graphy	writing	photography, geography

1. An unforeseen benefit of the new airport was a jump in foreign investment.
   Planners knew the project would attract overseas investors. (True / False)

2. Since the cloth makes light bend around it, it can make an object invisible.
   When the cloth is wrapped around something, anyone can see it. (True / False)

3. This biography of Gandhi is truly fascinating.
   The contents of the book have to do with Gandhi's life. (True / False)

Grammar *Preposition + Adjective Clause*

Many adjective clauses start with *whom* or *which*. These clauses sometimes end in a preposition like *in, for,* etc. In formal English, the preposition is often placed at the head of the clause instead of at the end.

| Ex: Astronomy is a topic which I'm very interested in. |
| *or* Astronomy is a topic in which I'm very interested. |
| Ex: Ms. Zhang is the teacher whom you should speak to. |
| *or* Ms. Zhang is the teacher to whom you should speak. |

Combine the sentences. (Place the preposition at the head of the adjective clause.)

1. It's a very difficult problem. There's no easy solution for it.

   _____

2. Car engines are a mystery. I know absolutely nothing about them.

   _____

3. You referred to a singer. She's a friend of my cousin's.

   _____

Talk About It   **Discuss these questions in small groups.**

1. If you could choose to see one idea from science fiction made into reality, what would it be?

2. Some people fear computers are getting too smart, too fast. Do super-intelligent machines frighten you? Why or why not?

3. Another concern is technology is making us lazy and unable to think for ourselves. Do you agree or disagree? Why?

Write About It

Question: Should national space agencies (like NASA) keep at least one full-time science fiction writer on staff? Give two reasons to support your opinion. Prepare by writing notes on the lines below. The first few words of the paragraph are written to help you get started.

Opinion: _____

Reason 1: _____

Reason 2: _____

Employing one or more science fiction writers would be _____

_____

_____

_____

_____

_____

_____

_____

Listening Listen to the speech. Then, answer the following questions.

🔊 Track 7

1. (   ) What is the purpose of this speech?
    (A) To demonstrate a product
    (B) To announce a breakthrough
    (C) To discuss a setback
    (D) To make a proposal

2. (   ) What does the speaker suggest about the X-Helmet?
    (A) It will be very expensive.
    (B) It took several decades to develop.
    (C) It has many applications.
    (D) It can be used without an X-Receiver.

3. (   ) Who is credited with the X-Helmet's success?
    (A) The military advisors   (B) The firm's executives
    (C) The research team   (D) The company's investors

Reading Choose the correct word(s) to fill in each blank.

The world contains an ample supply of creative new inventions. The question is, how many people want to risk (___1___) them out? Typically, inventors are the first in line. Given adequate safety precautions, the latest attempts at wearable computers and flying cars can be field tested with minimal risk. (___2___), when it comes to medical devices, stricter regulations are in place. For instance, firms have already created microscopic robots designed for internal therapies, and some animal tests have been carried out. Yet, tests involving injecting a person with such a device are another matter altogether. One reason advances like this take so long to reach market is because careful (___3___) must be followed before human subjects can participate in the testing stage.

1. (   ) (A) test   (B) to test
        (C) testing   (D) tested

2. (   ) (A) Therefore   (B) Coincidentally
        (C) Alternatively   (D) However

3. (   ) (A) procedures   (B) rejections
        (C) consequences   (D) inventions

Supplementary Reading - *Star Trek*

 Track 8

It would be hard to find a work of science fiction with a greater real-world impact than *Star Trek*. The futuristic television show, created by Gene Roddenberry, debuted in the USA in 1966. While creating exciting stories about "strange new worlds and new civilizations," Roddenberry used the space drama to comment on social and ethical issues.

The crew of the starship Enterprise was racially diverse, a landmark achievement in the 1960s. Working together, they used reason, compassion, and determination to solve problems while exploring the unknown. Of course, as the show took place hundreds of years in the future, the crew possessed an endless supply of fantastic weapons and devices. Many of these creations went on to influence real-world medical, military, communication, and other inventions.

The original series aired for just three seasons, but fan interest steadily grew, leading to the release of a cartoon series in the 1970s. That was followed by a number of live action movies. Then, in 1987, a brand new television series set in the *Star Trek* universe debuted. Even after Gene Roddenberry's death in 1991, more TV series and movies were made. Eventually, the franchise was "rebooted" with the 2009 blockbuster film simply entitled *Star Trek*.

Over the decades, the franchise has stayed true to Roddenberry's vision. *Star Trek* continues to address important issues such as medical ethics, disease, and war. So, despite taking place in the distant future, each *Star Trek* movie and TV show has something to say about the world we live in now.

Read each sentence. Circle if it is true (T) or false (F).

1. The original *Star Trek* TV show was set in the late 20th century.   T / F
2. A number of ideas from the show have led to actual inventions.   T / F
3. A new *Star Trek* live action TV show was filmed in the 1970s.   T / F
4. More than one film based on *Star Trek* has been produced.   T / F
5. The show rarely attempts to link story lines with real-world issues.   T / F

3 Business

Exporting Labor

In the global economy, millions of laborers travel abroad to work. People usually do so because of limited job opportunities at home. Though the money they send back helps their families, the system doesn't solve the long-term problems facing their home economies.

Pre-Reading Questions   Discuss these questions in pairs.

1. Which countries send a lot of workers overseas?

2. What kinds of jobs do they do?

3. What difficulties do people face when working overseas?

Vocabulary Warmup Track 9

A **Listen to the unit's target vocabulary. Then, write the letter of the correct word or phrase next to each definition.**

a. at (something's) core	f. drawback	k. per capita
b. child rearing	g. expatriate	l. sputter
c. compel	h. immune to	m. toil
d. concerted	i. initially	n. underlying
e. counseling	j. linguistic	o. unscrupulous

___ 1. dishonest

___ 2. citizen of one country who lives in another

___ 3. related to language

___ 4. at first; in the beginning

___ 5. at the heart of something

___ 6. focused; intensive

___ 7. work very hard

___ 8. unaffected by

___ 9. advice; therapy

___ 10. disadvantage; weakness

B **Complete each sentence with a target word or phrase. Remember to use the correct word form.**

1. Poverty is a(n) _____ cause of crime in the district.

2. After John's sister died, John felt _____ to adopt and raise his nephew.

3. When a country's economy _____, people expect the government to step in and improve things.

4. _____ income is usually higher in cities than in rural areas.

5. In families in which the husband and wife both work, _____ responsibilities are often shared between them.

Reading Passage Track 10

1   "Who are you?" This innocent question was asked by a little girl in the
Philippines. She wasn't talking to a new classmate or teacher. The question
was directed at her father, an engineer who had spent 10 years working in
Saudi Arabia. The man spent so little time with his family that his daughter
5   didn't even recognize him. He is one of the millions of people who have left
their families behind to work abroad. Whereas labor exporting countries can
benefit from the practice, it also has serious **drawbacks**.

Every region has countries which, because of high unemployment rates,
experience labor flights. In Central America, Mexico and Nicaragua are
10 significant labor exporters. In the Middle East, Lebanon and Jordan are top
sources of workers. And in Asia, India and
the Philippines are among the many labor
exporting countries. Top destinations tend to
be in the same region, for cultural, **linguistic**,
15 and other reasons. However, if the salary is
attractive enough, workers will contract to
work a great distance from home. Common
industries include construction, shipping,
factory work, health care, and **child rearing**.

*Overseas workers leave their homes to
provide a better life for their families.*

20 Financial considerations are the primary reasons for working abroad.
Typically, **expatriates** send a large percentage of their salaries home in the
form of remittances. The money benefits family members who, by buying
things locally, also help their communities. These remittances can be a
critical source of income. In 2008, overseas Filipinos sent home $16.4 billion,
25 representing 11.6% of the country's GDP. Similarly, in Nicaragua, incoming
remittances totaled 13% of GDP in 2008.

However, there are problems with the labor exporting system. First are the
costs. It's very expensive to go through an agency to set up the contract and

---

3 directed at – targeted at; meant for
9 labor flight – situation in which many workers leave a place
20 consideration – factor; reason
22 remittance – money sent back to one's home country
25 GDP – gross domestic product (the value of goods and services produced by a nation)

necessary paperwork. In Vietnam, these fees are between $2,500-$3,000,
30 a fortune compared to the yearly **per capita** income of $1,024. Additional
fees include applying for a passport and obtaining a health certificate.
What's more, a percentage of workers' earnings go to the agency. Some are
unscrupulous, taking advantage of workers by making them pay fees that
weren't **initially** agreed to.

35 Working conditions can also be problematic. It's not uncommon for laborers
to **toil** 12-18 hours a day. In extreme cases, they suffer emotional, physical,
or sexual abuse at the hands of their bosses. In 2009, Uganda barred women
from working as maids in a number of countries after a 24-year-old woman
returned home from Iraq. She had experienced severe physical abuse. In
40 response to cases like these, governments and private groups have set up
support centers. For example, Migrante International provides **counseling**
and legal assistance for Filipinos working overseas.

At their core, the **underlying** factors **compelling** labor migration need to
be considered. Countries usually view the system as a short-term fix for
45 economic problems. The hope is that as the domestic economy improves,
workers will return home. Yet without **concerted** government and industry
efforts to develop the local economy, countries tend to remain in poverty.
Nations also experience a "brain drain" in which their best-educated citizens
go abroad. A study by the Scalabrini Migration Center interviewed a group
50 of Filipina women who had traveled overseas to work. Some 50% were
college-educated, yet they left their country to work as maids or perform
other non-skilled tasks.

Finally, the overseas labor market is not **immune to** global downturns. In
2009, as several Middle Eastern economies **sputtered**, thousands of foreign
55 workers were sent home. Such downturns can severely affect countries
like India, which has some five million workers in the Persian Gulf. Still,
the trend to export laborers is expected to grow, thanks to the ongoing
integration of the global economy. As that happens, it's important that the
rights of workers be protected, both by the sending and receiving countries.

---

[30] fortune – large amount of money
[33] take advantage of – cheat; treat unfairly
[37] bar – prevent; ban
[58] integration – linking together; interconnecting

Reading Comprehension Choose the best answer.

.... **Main Idea**

1. ( ) What is the main idea?
   A. Overseas laborers tend to look for work in nearby countries.
   B. The Middle East and Asia both contain labor exporting countries.
   C. Though millions of people work abroad, the practice has drawbacks.
   D. Remittances are a major source of income in the Philippines.

.... **Detail**

2. ( ) The remittances made by Nicaraguans in 2008 totaled _____ of GDP.
   A. 11.6%   B. 13.0%
   C. 16.4%   D. 50.0%

.... **Vocabulary**

3. ( ) In line 10, what does "significant" mean?
   A. important   B. regional
   C. resourceful   D. indicated

.... **Analysis**

4. ( ) How are private agencies responding to overseas workers' problems?
   A. They're refusing to allow people to work in problematic countries.
   B. They're paying workers an additional sum for their troubles.
   C. They're supplying services to help workers deal with their issues.
   D. They're suing the agencies that arranged the contracts.

5. ( ) Why is the export of labor only a short-term fix for an economy?
   A. It doesn't provide any immediate benefits to families.
   B. Governments only allow people to work abroad for several years.
   C. By itself, the practice doesn't solve a nation's underlying problems.
   D. Communities are unable to send enough people overseas.

Short Answers Answer each question based on the article.

1. What problem do Vietnamese laborers face if they want to work overseas?

   _____

2. In 2009, why did Uganda bar women from working as maids in several countries?

   _____

3. What happens to overseas workers during global economic downturns?

   _____

Vocabulary Building

A **Choose the answer that means the same as the word in italics.**

1. The shopping mall is known for having *unscrupulous* stores which try to cheat tourists.
   A. competitive   B. emotional   C. dishonest

2. A *concerted* cleanup effort made the once-polluted river sparkle again.
   A. environmental   B. intensive   C. suggested

3. One *drawback* to relying on the Internet is businesses suffer when their Net access is interrupted.
   A. advantage   B. limitation   C. remedy

4. Jeff's father *toiled* in a coal mine for 30 years to provide for his family.
   A. managed   B. invested   C. labored

5. Factory pollution is an *underlying* cause of global warming.
   A. underrated   B. supplemental   C. primary

B **Complete each sentence with the best word or phrase. Remember to use the correct word form.**

| counseling | immune to | per capita | expatriate | child rearing |

1. Sam is _____ the effects of the weather. Even the coldest winters don't bother him.

2. _____, which involves cleaning, cooking, washing, and more, is a full-time job.

3. A lot of Italian _____ like this restaurant since its food is just like the cusine back home.

4. People who have been in serious accidents may require _____ before they're ready to return to work.

5. Thanks to strong exports, _____ income rose last year.

C **Circle the correct form of each word.**

1. Due to the recent storm, the (initial/initially) completion date may need to be revised.

2. (Linguistic/Linguistically), Germany and Austria have a lot in common.

3. (Compelling/Compelled) people to work over the holiday will not be easy.

4. (At its core/At their core), the Hollywood film industry is about producing films that millions of people want to see.

5. The (sputter/sputtering) housing market is expected to recover next year.

Part 2: Focus Areas

Focus on Language

Word Parts

Study the word parts in the chart. Then, read the following pairs of sentences. Circle if the second sentence is true or false.

Word Part	Meaning	Examples
prim-	first	primal, primer
-cogn-	know	recognition, cognitive
-back	return	fallback, comeback

1. Our primary goal should be to strengthen the bridge's support pillars.
   Making the pillars stronger is the main task. (True / False)

2. The star walked around incognito so people wouldn't bother her.
   She wore a disguise to avoid being recognized. (True / False)

3. Despite the setbacks, we're confident the play will be a success.
   The problems with the production will probably cause it to fail. (True / False)

Grammar   Whereas vs. Whereby

Whereas is used to introduce an adverb clause. It means "while" and is used in a sentence comparing two things. *Whereby* is an adverb meaning "by which." It introduces a clause which says more about a noun.

Ex: Whereas Jennifer is a soccer fan, her sister prefers volleyball.

Ex: Photosynthesis is the process whereby a flower converts sunlight into energy.

Complete each sentence with *whereas* or *whereby*.

1. *A Brief History of Time* was the book _____ Stephen Hawking became a household name.

2. I voted to change the club's name to "The Blue Wanderers," _____ Jim voted to keep the old name.

3. _____ it's too small for an orchard, the plot would make a great flower garden.

4. I'm learning about the method _____ bags are made waterproof.

Talk About It   **Discuss these questions in small groups.**

1. In your country, how are international workers treated? Do they have a good life?

2. What can be done to help overseas workers who suffer from physical abuse or other problems?

3. How can labor exporting countries improve conditions at home so their citizens don't need to travel abroad to work?

Write About It

Question: From the point of view of workers, is the current overseas labor system fair or unfair? Give two reasons to support your opinion. Prepare by writing notes on the lines below. The first few words of the paragraph are written to help you get started.

Opinion: _____

Reason 1: _____

Reason 2: _____

In general, I believe the current system is _____

_____

_____

_____

_____

_____

_____

_____

_____

Listening Listen to the conversation. Then, answer the following questions.

Track 11

1. (   ) Who is Mr. Richards?
   (A) A Mexican travel agent
   (B) A friend of Tom's
   (C) A relative of Sue's
   (D) An insurance firm manager

2. (   ) What did Sue say after receiving the offer?
   (A) She couldn't accept the position.
   (B) She would start in seven days.
   (C) She needed to think things over.
   (D) She was ready immediately.

3. (   ) What does Tom think Sue's biggest problem would be?
   (A) Salary issues
   (B) Language problems
   (C) Family matters
   (D) Experience concerns

Reading Read the article. Then, answer the following questions.

While many firms become conservative during economic downturns, others go on the offensive. In 2009 that's exactly what Stanford Construction did. As the housing industry sputtered, most construction firms saw a steep decline in new home orders. Stanford was not immune to the downturn, yet instead of laying off staff, the company shifted its focus. They reasoned that few homeowners were willing to upgrade to larger, more expensive properties, yet they might be interested in renovating their current homes. So, Stanford put together a range of affordable plans, with lower material costs allowing them to offer great deals. Thanks to a concerted effort by their employees, the firm managed to grow 5% during an otherwise miserable year for the sector.

1. (   ) What is this article mainly about?
   (A) The global financial crisis of 2009
   (B) Modern techniques for renovating homes
   (C) Cyclical industries of the 21st century
   (D) A story of success in the face of adversity

2. (   ) How did Stanford Construction respond to the industry downturn?
   (A) It became conservative.
   (B) It took a new approach.
   (C) It borrowed a large sum.
   (D) It fired several employees.

3. (   ) What was NOT an ingredient in Stanford's achievement?
   (A) An all-out staff effort
   (B) Cheaper building components
   (C) Shrewd market analysis
   (D) The acquisition of a competitor

Supplementary Reading - *The Case of Dubai* Track 12

In the 2000s, Dubai's super-fast growth captured the world's attention. The commercial center of the United Arab Emirates (UAE), Dubai has become known for luxury hotels like the Burj Al Arab, shopping paradises like the Mall of the Emirates, and bold architectural feats like the 828-meter-tall Burj Khalifa. The city's population grew from just over one million residents in 2002 to 6.4 million in 2007. Of that, the vast majority were expatriates.

This cosmopolitan oasis was largely built by foreign laborers from countries like India and Bangladesh. Indeed, in 2007 they made up more than three million of the 5.5 million foreign residents. These laborers fixed steel girders hundreds of meters up, laid brick several stories high, and painted walls on street level. The arrangement worked out well for both sides, as the expat workers earned up  to several thousand US dollars per month. The remittances they sent home were a boon to their families and hometown economies.

Yet when the global financial system crashed in 2008, even mighty Dubai was hard hit. Real estate values plummeted, and many construction projects were delayed or cancelled. The situation got so bad that Dubai World, the state-owned enterprise behind many building projects, needed an emergency cash infusion from neighboring Abu Dhabi to help pay its debts. Dubai's downturn also led to mass lay-offs of foreign laborers. Planes leaving the city were full of workers leaving the desert paradise they had helped build.

Read each sentence. Circle if it is true (T) or false (F).

1. Many of Dubai's skyscrapers were built in the mid-20th century.   T / F
2. From 2002 to 2007, Dubai's population grew by about five million.   T / F
3. Dubai benefited from its foreign labor pool, but the workers themselves did not see much gain.   T / F
4. Dubai World was a structure built by investors from Abu Dhabi.   T / F
5. Many foreign workers lost their jobs as a result of Dubai's economic problems.   T / F

The Environment

Celebrating the Earth

Environmental news has dominated headlines for more than a decade.
One way people are helping improve the environment is through positive
celebrations of the Earth. Actions include joining harvest festivals,
participating in Earth Day activities, and supporting environmental groups.

Pre-Reading Questions Discuss these questions in pairs.

1. What do people do on Earth Day?

2. What are some big non-profit environmental groups? What do they do?

3. In our daily lives, how can we help the environment?

Vocabulary Warmup Track 13

A **Listen to the unit's target vocabulary. Then, write the letter of the correct word or phrase next to each definition.**

a. appliance	f. endangered	k. politician
b. coincide with	g. from the outset	l. spearhead
c. collectively	h. harvest	m. take root
d. constructive	i. in the face of	n. urbanization
e. contribution	j. legislation	o. vital

____ 1. lead; direct

____ 2. assistance; support

____ 3. law

____ 4. gathering of the crops

____ 5. very important

____ 6. growth of cities and city life

____ 7. at risk of becoming extinct

____ 8. since the beginning

____ 9. all together

____ 10. lawmaker; member of the government

B **Complete each sentence with a target word or phrase. Remember to use the correct word form.**

1. I hope the habit of recycling batteries will _____ someday. Everyone should properly dispose of their used batteries.

2. Not only is the refrigerator a common home _____, but it's also one of the biggest energy users.

3. Several _____ suggestions were made about how we might reduce air pollution.

4. _____ so much debt and competition, the furniture store was forced to go out of business.

5. The Earth Day march will _____ the start of the Bike to Work campaign.

Part 1: Reading and Vocabulary Building

1   News reports about the environment often focus on rising temperatures, melting glaciers, and disappearing forests. **In the face of** a long train of bad news, it's easy to feel frustrated or powerless. However, there is a lot we can do to make positive **contributions** to the environment. These efforts

5   are highlighted by local and global celebrations of the Earth. They raise awareness about important issues while providing **constructive** ideas for making our lives greener.

Most cultures are strongly connected to the Earth through agricultural traditions. For thousands of years, societies have celebrated the **harvest's**

10 importance, and many holidays take place in the summer or fall to **coincide with** the harvest season. Some examples are Sukkot (Israel), Pongal (India), and Chuseok (Korea). Despite the trend towards **urbanization** and the growing importance of technology, we still take time to honor

15 the Earth through festivals like these.

In India, Pongal celebrates the harvest and the cow, which is considered sacred.

In modern times, an international holiday has **taken root**: Earth Day. The first Earth Day was held in the USA on April 22, 1970. **From the outset**, it was a huge success, attracting 20 million participants. The

20 event, designed to make **politicians** aware of voters' concerns about the environment, yielded excellent results. Shortly after the event, the US government created the Environmental Protection Agency, which went on to **spearhead** important **legislation** like the Clean Air Act (1970),

25 Clean Water Act (1972), and Food Quality Protection Act (1996).

Within a few years, Earth Day grew to include nearly every country on the planet. The Earth Day Network, a group which coordinates activities

---

2 glacier – a very large, slow-moving mass of ice
5 highlight – bring attention to; provide a good example of
5 raise awareness – inform people about something to get them interested
27 coordinate – organize; arrange

30 on and around the holiday, now has partners in 174 countries. Every year, thousands of events are held to raise environmental awareness and celebrate the Earth through music, dance, and art. Past events include a cleanup of part of the River Thames in London and a bike riding festival in Moscow. In Beijing, the 2007 "Bye-bye throw-away culture" week brought attention to the damage caused by plastic bags. Months later, the Chinese government passed a law banning the distribution of thin plastic bags.

35 Beyond this special holiday, there are many groups working non-stop on the planet's behalf. They raise awareness about **vital** issues and get people involved in Earth-friendly activities. One, the World Wildlife Fund, has worked hard since 1961 to protect **endangered** species like the panda bear and mountain gorilla. Another important group is the Sierra Club, founded
40 in 1892. It reaches out to the public through its website, which has tips for setting up a "Green Living Tips" workshop. People can download all the videos, flyers, and information they need to host a "going green" party.

One of the best ways to celebrate the Earth is by making small changes in our lives. Several relate to our homes, such as purchasing energy-efficient
45 light bulbs and **appliances**. Others involve daily habits, such as buying locally grown food, recycling, and using public transportation. The Earth Day Network runs a "Billion Acts of Green" campaign which encourages people to take small steps and, if they wish, share their experiences online. The idea is that, **collectively**, small-scale Earth-friendly activities can make
50 a big difference.

Of course, what better way to enjoy nature than by taking a walk, hike, or bike ride with friends and family members. Climbing mountains, swimming in lakes, and walking through forests can be powerful reminders of what we're fighting to save. Thanks to the hard work of volunteers,
55 organizers, and community leaders, many beautiful places have been preserved for future generations. Now that's something to smile about.

---

40 reach out – contact; make a connection
40 tip – idea; suggestion
42 flyer – information sheet
47 campaign – movement; focused effort
56 preserve – maintain; protect

Choose the best answer.

.... **Main Idea**

1. ( ) What is the main idea?
   A. There's very little any of us can do to help the Earth.
   B. Positive efforts supporting the environment are having a global impact.
   C. It's fun to celebrate harvest festivals in the autumn.
   D. Earth Day has been a huge success since its creation four decades ago.

.... **Detail**

2. ( ) What does the Earth Day Network do?
   A. It introduces legislation for world governments to consider.
   B. It coordinates activities for groups like the Sierra Club.
   C. It runs contests to see who can arrange a billion activities first.
   D. It assists in setting up plans related to Earth Day events.

.... **Vocabulary**

3. ( ) In line 21, what does "yielded" mean?
   A. led to   B. came from
   C. hoped for   D. relied on

.... **Analysis**

4. ( ) What can be inferred about urbanization?
   A. It hasn't erased people's interest in harvest festivals.
   B. Its impact is as important as that of technology.
   C. The trend has influenced India more than Israel.
   D. Few people are concerned about its effects on the Earth.

5. ( ) What does the article imply about buying locally grown food?
   A. It's one of many ways to support the environment.
   B. Doing so is cheaper than buying imported food.
   C. The practice was first made popular on Earth Day.
   D. It does more to help the Earth than recycling.

Short Answers **Answer each question based on the article.**

1. What are the names and locations of two harvest festivals?

   _____

2. What was the immediate result of the first Earth Day?

   _____

3. What was the positive impact of the "Bye-bye throw-away culture" week?

   _____

Vocabulary Building

A Choose the answer that means the same as the word or phrase in italics.

1. *From the outset*, Yahoo has been one of the world's most famous companies.
   A. From the start   B. In recent times   C. Years from now

2. Hideki is the perfect person to *spearhead* the forest restoration campaign.
   A. overrun   B. overturn   C. oversee

3. The restaurant's half-price special will *coincide with* the start of the Olympics.
   A. fortify with   B. alternate with   C. correspond with

4. Family-run stores have to work hard *in the face of* competition from large chain stores.
   A. regardless of   B. compared to   C. up against

5. *Appliances* like microwave ovens are commonplace in today's kitchens.
   A. Luxury goods   B. Decorative items   C. Electrical devices

B Complete each sentence with the best word or phrase. Remember to use the correct word form.

| harvest | take root | urbanization | politician | endangered |

1. In the age of mass media, _____ spend a lot of time on television discussing their positions and campaigning for votes.

2. Since interest in organic food has _____, more and more organic produce shops are opening.

3. Thanks to conservation efforts, some _____ species have rebounded and are once again thriving.

4. In the fall, the villagers work together to gather the _____.

5. Over the last 50 years, _____ has led to the growth of huge cities.

C Circle the correct form of each word.

1. (Contributions/Contributors) from four continents write material for the travel blog.

2. It's (vital/vitally) that you tell the police everything you saw.

3. In a (collective/collectively) effort, the farmers built a canal to the river.

4. Taking (legislative/legislate) action is a long process requiring thorough analysis and deliberation.

5. Instead of placing blame, let's try to deal with the traffic problem (constructive/constructively) and come up with a solution.

37

Part 2: Focus Areas

Focus on Language

Word Parts

Study the word parts in the chart. Then, read the following pairs of sentences. Circle if the second sentence is true or false.

Word Part	Meaning	Examples
agr(i)-	related to land	agrarian, agrichemical
-port-	carry; ship	export, deported
-ity	degree; position	capacity, irregularity

1. Agribusiness is a core industry in both Johnson and Shepherd Counties.
   The counties rely on the local production of gloves, hats, etc. (True / False)

2. Let's take the portable heater with us in case it gets cold.
   The heater is difficult to carry from one place to another. (True / False)

3. When Ted saw the Burj Khalifa, he was shocked by its immensity.
   Ted was surprised by the size of the building. (True / False)

Grammar   *What better way...than by*

This structure is used to express the best way to do something. The phrase *what better way* is followed by the goal, after which the solution is given.
Structure: **what better way + infinitive + than by + v-ing**
Ex: What better way to say thank you than by sending a box of chocolates.
Ex: What better way to get the job done than by going to Italy yourself.

Rewrite the second sentence using *what better way...than by*.

1. A: How should I repay the favor?   B: You should buy Jack dinner.

   _____

2. A: How can I make Cindy believe me?   B: Tell her exactly what happened.

   _____

3. A: How can I learn about farming?   B: Maybe you can plant a garden.

   _____

Talk About It · **Discuss these questions in small groups.**

1. In general, do you find the news about the environment (in newspapers, on television, etc.) positive or negative? How does the news make you feel?

2. What types of Earth Day events would you like to participate in?

3. Some environmental groups take extreme measures like lying down in front of bulldozers. Are these techniques effective? Do you agree with them?

Write About It

Question: Who should lead the effort to improve the environment: governments, individuals, or non-profit organizations? Give two reasons to support your opinion. Prepare by writing notes on the lines below. The first few words of the paragraph are written to help you get started.

Opinion: _____

Reason 1: _____

Reason 2: _____

To improve the environment, we need leadership from

_____

_____

_____

_____

_____

_____

_____

Listening

Track 15

Listen to the speech. Then, answer the following questions.

1. ( ) Who is the intended audience?
   (A) Government officials
   (B) Farming advocates
   (C) Financial donors
   (D) Urban planners

2. ( ) What has happened to Vietnam's forests in recent years?
   (A) Most of them have been restored.
   (B) All of them have been protected.
   (C) Many of them have been cleared.
   (D) Few of them have been cut down.

3. ( ) What type of land does the group want to acquire?
   (A) Previously forested lands
   (B) Downtown urban properties
   (C) Offshore marine areas
   (D) Currently thriving woodlands

Reading   **Choose the correct word(s) to fill in each blank.**

Since 1987, Claudia Zimmer has spearheaded recycling efforts in her small town. As it includes less than 10,000 (__1__), community activities are typically driven by such grassroots efforts. Ms. Zimmer turned her attention to the environment after watching a documentary on landfills in the mid-1980s. From the outset, she was committed to the task, and her enthusiasm attracted several friends to the cause. They (__2__) recycling centers throughout the town for common items like plastic bottles and newspapers. Later, their scope expanded to include furniture, appliances, and other household items. Many electrical goods are repaired and redistributed, (__3__) articles of clothing are given to local charities. Items which can't be reused are recycled.

1. ( ) (A) residential
      (C) residing
      (B) residentially
      (D) residents

2. ( ) (A) brought up
      (C) rose up
      (B) set up
      (D) caught up

3. ( ) (A) while
      (C) since
      (B) for
      (D) after

Supplementary Reading - *Greenpeace*

 Track 16

Greenpeace has become synonymous with environmental activism. Since its founding in 1971, the group has captured international headlines with bold, uncompromising campaigns. Their first action, designed to prevent underground nuclear testing off the coast of Alaska, soon led to the end of further testing in the area. Since then, they have campaigned on numerous issues, including protecting forest and marine areas, ending the use of toxic chemicals in consumer products, and stopping the production of genetically engineered crops. Several high-profile decisions made by international firms, governments, and the UN can be directly linked to Greenpeace campaigns.

The group, headquartered in Amsterdam, is funded by private contributions from its 2.8 million members. Greenpeace uses non-violent protest methods to carry out its goals. For instance, its fleet of boats, led by the flagship vessel Rainbow Warrior, identifies and blockades toxic waste dumpers and illegal fishing boats. They often unfurl large banners which, when captured on camera, make for dramatic news reports. That's intentional, as campaigns can generate momentum once they attract enough public attention.

Greenpeace also organizes parades, signature gathering campaigns, and Internet-based efforts. Plus, it finances scientific research, leading to important breakthroughs like Greenfreeze, an environmentally friendly refrigerator. Yet the group is not without its critics. Some call their actions extremist and counterproductive, while others say the non-profit organization worries too much about publicity. Whichever stance one takes, Greenpeace's impact on legislation, company policies, and public awareness over the last four decades is hard to deny.

Read each sentence. Circle if it is true (T) or false (F).

1. Greenpeace's first action was part of a campaign to save a forest. T / F
2. One of their goals is to improve the safety of consumer goods. T / F
3. Greenpeace has nearly three million members around the world. T / F
4. Greenfreeze resulted from legislation that can be linked to a Greenpeace campaign. T / F
5. The group has been criticized for trying too hard to grab headlines. T / F

The Internet

5

Virtual Lives

The Internet is not just providing tools that make our lives easier. It's even starting to act as a replacement for reality. Online forums, social networking sites, and virtual worlds are being used by schools, businesses, and artists. Yet our online identities tend to be distinct from our offline personas.

Pre-Reading Questions   Discuss these questions in pairs.

1. Are you a member of any social networking sites (like Facebook)?

2. Have you ever participated as a character in a 3D world? (ex: an online game or virtual world)

3. What advantages might businesses enjoy by holding meetings or conferences in a virtual world (as opposed to meeting in person)?

Vocabulary Warmup Track 17

A Listen to the unit's target vocabulary. Then, write the letter of the correct word or phrase next to each definition.

a. avatar	f. extension	k. restraint
b. coincidence	g. facet	l. sheer
c. conduct	h. fickle	m. socialize
d. enhance	i. illustrate	n. stake (one's) claim
e. envelop	j. out of favor	o. venue

___ 1. improve

___ 2. aspect; element

___ 3. meet and talk with people

___ 4. location

___ 5. show; demonstrate

___ 6. assert one's right to something

___ 7. addition; expansion

___ 8. no longer popular or supported

___ 9. completely cover or encircle

___ 10. limitation; restriction

B Complete each sentence with a target word or phrase. Remember to use the correct word form.

1. The _____ size of the Eiffel Tower is impressive.

2. Police say it was not a(n) _____ that the suspect was in the building at the time of the murder.

3. Marcia is somewhat _____, so you might want to confirm your plans before driving across town to meet her.

4. In virtual worlds, people sometimes create _____ which look exactly like them.

5. We'd like to _____ the interview in Conference Room B, but it's fully booked for the day.

Part 1: Reading and Vocabulary Building

1   In many **facets** of life, the Internet's importance is unmistakable. From **socializing** to doing business to conducting research, the Net has reached out and, literally, **enveloped** us in its web. Increasingly, as people spend more time on the Net, they're virtually living online. There are even 3D

5   worlds in which people can walk, talk, and shop, just as they do in the "real world." This **extension** of reality, in which people look and act any way they want, could have a profound impact on our concepts of identity.

   The **sheer** variety of online spaces makes it tricky to define Internet usage patterns. Social networking sites like Facebook attract hundreds of millions

10   of users. There are also more than 100 million blogs, where people **stake their claim** to a small corner of the Net. On top of that, there are countless forums, chatrooms, and message boards where people meet to share common interests. Yet the Internet is, if anything, **fickle**, and what's popular today may be **out of favor** tomorrow. In a sense, one's online identity,

15   because it isn't tied to any one space, is flexible and transient.

   There are also virtual worlds which bring together common functions like social networking, chatting, and image sharing. One of the most well known, Second Life, was started in 2003 by Linden Lab. To participate, members create a 3D character, known as an **avatar**, which represents the

20   user. The avatar walks, flies, or teleports to diverse locations in a vast online world, where popular activities include shopping, visiting art galleries, and going to clubs. If this sounds like an **enhanced** version of the real world, that's not a **coincidence**. Linden Lab's CEO, Phillip Rosedale, states, "Our goal with Second Life is to make it better than real life in a lot of ways."

25   Indeed, people are using the application for practical uses. Universities such as Harvard Law School are holding classes in Second Life. When it's time for class, students simply log on and direct their avatars into a classroom. They

---

[1] unmistakable – clear; obvious
[8] tricky – difficult; not easy to do
[15] flexible – changeable; able to adapt
[15] transient – temporary; not staying in one place

can participate via text or voice chat. Some schools are using the world as a "testing ground" to **illustrate** real-world principles. For instance, in one marketing class, the teacher has students set up a retail store. There, they witness how people react to their surroundings, what types of displays work best, etc. This type of hands-on experience would be difficult to **conduct** offline, due to cost **restraints** and practicality issues.

Commercial uses for virtual worlds are also being explored. In Second Life, people can buy goods using the site's virtual currency – the Linden dollar (which can be purchased using a real credit card). Companies are also finding it cost-efficient to transfer certain operations online. In 2008 IBM held a Virtual World Conference in Second Life. The event featured three keynote speeches as well as 37 smaller presentations, and more than 200 people participated. The firm saved $320,000 by hosting the conference online instead of at a traditional **venue**. Intel similarly held its 2009 virtual ECC conference on the site. The cost savings ($265,000) were also impressive.

Virtual meetings and conferences save companies a fortune.

Bit by bit, more activities are shifting to the Internet, raising important questions about the nature of online identity. Indeed, if the sites we visit grow and shrink in popularity in a matter of years (or even months), people can't experience the same type of "rooting" traditionally enjoyed in offline communities. Also, as online friends quickly come and go, what does that say about our ability to form lasting, meaningful relationships? As we live a growing percentage of our lives on the Internet, concepts like friendship, community, and self-image may need to be refined, or perhaps entirely redefined.

---

29 principle – point; concept
31 surroundings – environment; setting
32 hands-on – practical; active
35 currency – money
40 keynote speech – an important speech at a conference

Choose the best answer.

........Main Idea

1. ( ) What is the main idea?
   A. Second Life is an interesting and useful website.
   B. Businesses save a lot of money by holding events on the Internet.
   C. People spend so much time online that it's changing our lives.
   D. Virtual worlds are more interactive than blogs.

........Detail

2. ( ) How did IBM make use of Second Life?
   A. They set up a research and development lab there.
   B. They hired 200 Second Life members to work for IBM.
   C. They made the website the location of a conference.
   D. They presented 37 new product ideas on the site.

........Vocabulary

3. ( ) In line 31, what does "witness" mean?
   A. testify   B. conduct
   C. comment   D. observe

........Analysis

4. ( ) What does the article imply about the Internet?
   A. Online trends come and go very quickly.
   B. The Internet makes it easy to form lasting friendships.
   C. Younger people spend the most time on the Net.
   D. The number of chatrooms is starting to shrink.

5. ( ) What aspect of Second Life is not discussed in the article?
   A. Business opportunities   B. Real estate management
   C. Educational purposes   D. Entertainment options

Short Answers   Answer each question based on the article.

1. Why is it difficult to define Internet usage patterns?

_____

2. How do avatars in Second Life move around?

_____

3. Why is it difficult to create offline "testing grounds"?

_____

Vocabulary Building

A **Choose the answer that means the same as the word or phrase in italics.**

1. During the dust storm, the city was *enveloped* in a cloud of yellow dirt.
   A. covered   B. polluted   C. breached

2. Since last year's *venue* was too small, they're moving this year's event to the new convention center.
   A. participation   B. location   C. expectation

3. During the press conference, we'll discuss several *facets* of the merger.
   A. reasons   B. promises   C. aspects

4. Large cars are *out of favor*, due to environmental concerns and high oil costs.
   A. discontinued   B. reconsidered   C. unpopular

5. Time *restraints* forced us to limit speeches to five minutes each.
   A. limitations   B. objections   C. expansions

B **Complete each sentence with the best word or phrase. Remember to use the correct word form.**

socialize	fickle	sheer	stake one's claim	avatar

1. The "Come one, come all" event is a great chance to _____ with your classmates.

2. We were surprised by the _____ number of people who turned up at the demonstration.

3. I wouldn't say Stacey is _____, since I've found her to be reliable. However, she does take a while to make up her mind.

4. Sam is short, but in the game his _____ is 10 feet tall.

5. Darren, you should _____ to a chair before they're all taken.

C **Circle the correct form of each word.**

1. Rita and I went shopping at Westfield Mall this afternoon. (Coincidence/ Coincidentally), we bumped into Jessica on the way out.

2. I think Dr. Leister's (illustrate/illustration) of the M-shaped model, as it relates to Eastern Europe, is brilliant.

3. The new multimedia wing will lead to a marked (enhancement/enhance) of library visitors' experiences.

4. They're (extension/extending) the tour since it has been so successful.

5. We're planning to (conduct/conductor) the meeting in English and French.

Part 2: Focus Areas

Focus on Language

Word Parts

Study the word parts in the chart. Then, read the following pairs of sentences. Circle if the second sentence is true or false.

Word Part	Meaning	Examples
sur-	above; beyond	surplus, surpass
-cept-	receive	accept, deception
-ship	identity; state	friendship, partnership

1. Though wheelchair bound, Ivy surmounted her disability and became wealthy.
   The woman overcame her disability to achieve success. (True / False)

2. The movie has had a mixed reception, with critics both for and against it.
   There isn't widespread agreement about the film. (True / False)

3. Ownership over the disputed property will be settled in court.
   The legal owner of the property has been determined. (True / False)

Grammar   *What's...may be*

This structure is used to compare two ideas or attitudes about something. Prepositional phrases and adverbs can be inserted to add depth to the sentence.

Structure: **what's + adjective + may be + adjective**

Ex: What's popular in one country may be unknown in another.

Ex: What's unusual to you may be normal to someone in Mexico.

Write a response using *what's...may be*. The start of each sentence is given.

1. Sid found the math problem hard. Mario solved it in 10 seconds.
   What's difficult
   _____

2. I can get T-shirts in China for a dollar. They cost 10 times that in Miami.
   What's cheap
   _____

3. Some cell phones which are seen as new in the USA are old in Japan.
   What's considered new
   _____

Talk About It   **Discuss these questions in small groups.**

1. What do you feel are the best uses for a virtual world like Second Life? Meeting people? Working? Something else?

2. Do people behave differently online than in the "real world"? If so, how?

3. Children are spending more and more time online. How can we protect them from the dangers of the Internet?

Write About It

Question: In the future, will people spend the entire day online, from morning until night? Give two reasons to support your opinion. Prepare by writing notes on the lines below. The first few words of the paragraph are written to help you get started.

Opinion: _____

Reason 1: _____

Reason 2: _____

In the future, people will use the Internet _____

_____

_____

_____

_____

_____

_____

_____

Listening

Track 19

Listen to the conversation. Then, answer the following questions.

1. (   ) What does the man invite the woman to do?
    (A) Meet a new friend
    (B) Attend a wedding
    (C) Take a harbor cruise
    (D) Go to a party

2. (   ) Who hasn't the woman seen for a long time?
    (A) Mitch
    (B) Jennifer
    (C) Paul
    (D) Louise

3. (   ) What does the man suggest about Jennifer?
    (A) She frequently forgets things.
    (B) She is not trustworthy.
    (C) She is a serious person.
    (D) She often borrows money.

Reading   **Read the announcement. Then, answer the following questions.**

Greetings, fellow V-Worlders! Thanks to you, V-World is a great place to explore, with thousands of V-Centers providing everything from musical performances to retail outlets to lectures by leading scientists. The sheer number of opportunities is amazing, but we're still not done improving your virtual experience. On August 3, V-World 2.0 will launch. Many of you have said our avatars aren't distinctive enough, and we've been listening. One of the new features of V-World 2.0 will be a rebuilt avatar engine. You'll be able to import photographs and use them to create a 3D face or body. You'll also be able to add images to hats, shirts, and jackets. The idea is to enhance your avatar by personalizing it as much as you want.

1. (   ) Who is this announcement directed at?
    (A) Current V-Worlders
    (B) Website advertisers
    (C) All Internet users
    (D) Future V-Center builders

2. (   ) What type of V-Center is NOT discussed?
    (A) Commercial
    (B) Educational
    (C) Entertainment
    (D) Religious

3. (   ) What is implied about V-World's current avatars?
    (A) Images can be added to their hats.
    (B) They are in need of improvement.
    (C) Users can make them photo-realistic.
    (D) Most people like the way they look.

Supplementary Reading - *Growing up Online* Track 20

Whereas adults often look at the Internet as an external tool (be it for working, communicating, making friends, or finding information), a whole generation of children is literally growing up with the Net. For them, some of their earliest circles of friends are being formed online, and the Internet is not just an extension of their lives, but rather a central feature. Over time, this shift could have serious implications for the nature of personal identities and relationship building.

Thanks to smart phones and other wireless devices, many young people are constantly online, virtually sharing their lives in real time. Digital photos taken with cell phones can immediately be added to blogs, social networking sites, and message boards. Text messages, as well as the super-short messages posted on Twitter, also keep networks of friends up to date. This extremely brief form of communication is giving rise to a vocabulary full of acronyms, abbreviations, and other new terms. The trend could have long-term implications for the way people learn to write and express themselves.

The research group Nielsen has provided hard figures confirming the growth of the Internet generation in the USA. They found that from 2004 to 2009, the number of American kids (2-11 years old) online grew by 18% to reach 16 million. In comparison, during the same period, the number of American adults online grew by just 10%. What's more, in 2009, children in that age bracket spent an average of 11 hours per month online. That was more than a 50% increase over the 2004 average.

Read each sentence. Circle if it is true (T) or false (F).

1. Adults and children may have different outlooks about the Net.   T / F
2. There are few differences between online and offline relationship building.   T / F
3. Twitter and text messaging formats could affect people's general writing styles.   T / F
4. More than 16 million American kids used the Internet in 2004.   T / F
5. From 2004 to 2009, the number of American adults online shrank.   T / F

Growing and Aging

6

Kidults

For many people, the idea of what it means to be an adult is changing. More and more adults have "childlike" interests, such as playing video games and collecting toys. Companies are even producing children's style clothing and products specifically for adults.

Pre-Reading Questions   Discuss these questions in pairs.

1. At what age do people usually move out of their parents' home?

2. In general, are people growing up more slowly than they used to?

3. Are you interested in anything that is traditionally associated with childhood? (ex: toys, cartoons, comic books)

Vocabulary Warmup Track 21

A **Listen to the unit's target vocabulary. Then, write the letter of the correct word or phrase next to each definition.**

a. bluntly	f. indulge	k. ramification
b. cash in on	g. mature	l. remarkable
c. coin (a term)	h. mindset	m. stay put
d. disposable income	i. opt	n. steady
e. ignore	j. pros and cons	o. take heart

___ 1. remain in the same place

___ 2. invent a new word

___ 3. pay no attention to

___ 4. consequence

___ 5. directly; pointedly

___ 6. money available for leisure goods and other interests

___ 7. calm; stable

___ 8. way of thinking; mental state

___ 9. earn money from

___ 10. advantages and disadvantages

B **Complete each sentence with a target word or phrase. Remember to use the correct word form.**

1. Applicants can _____ from the news that there are enough job openings for everyone.

2. If George is so _____, why does he carry his food in a child's lunchbox?

3. When we reach the port, passengers may _____ to remain on board if they wish.

4. The buffet included a dessert bar, so we _____ ourselves with three pieces of cake.

5. The band gave a(n) _____ performance that had fans cheering and clapping the whole way through.

Part 1: Reading and Vocabulary Building

1   In 1983, Cyndi Lauper reached the top of the charts with her hit song "Girls Just Want to Have Fun." These days, the same could be said for millions of men and women in their 20s, 30s, and even 40s. These so-called "kidults" dress and behave like children. Refusing to grow up, they often live with
5   their parents, play video games, and watch cartoons. Observers point to positive and negative **ramifications** of the trend, which is all about having fun and avoiding, at all costs, the "R" word: Responsibility.

The word "kidult" is a combination of "kid" and "adult." (Other recently **coined** terms include "adultescent" and "rejuvenile.") Kidults often live with
10   their parents long after finishing high school and college. It's a fast-growing trend. In 1970, only 11% of American 26-year-olds lived with their parents, but by 2005, that figure had grown to 20%. Likewise, people are getting married and having children later. In Ireland, for instance, the average marriage age rose from 30.7 in 2000 to 32.6 in 2005.

15   Facts like these have led some observers to suggest that people are growing up later and later. Rather than finding a **steady** job, getting married, and taking out a mortgage, many people are **opting** for a different path. They're **staying put**, taking whatever work comes along, and devoting their **disposable income** to having a good time.

20   Consumerism plays a key role in the trend, as kidults' lack of financial obligations frees up money for electronic goods, cars, and clothes. Over the last decade, marketers have **cashed in on** the opportunity, with companies making toys and collectibles specifically for adults. Recently, in St. Petersburg, Russia, a television channel called 2x2 was created for
25   the young-at-heart. Featuring cartoons like *The Simpsons*, the channel tells viewers to "Switch off your brain. Switch on 2x2." Indeed, there's a constant marketing stream encouraging people to think less and, instead, enjoy life to

---

⁹ adultescent – combination of the words "adult" and "adolescent"
⁹ rejuvenile – an adult who acts like a child (literally: to become a juvenile again)
¹⁸ devote – commit
²⁰ consumerism – the habit of buying things
²¹ obligation – responsibility
²⁷ enjoy life to the brim – have as good a time as possible

the brim. Christopher Noxon, author of *Rejuvenile*, **bluntly** sums things up: "It has become unfashionable to be **mature**."

30 What are the **pros and cons** of being a kidult? On the one hand, people can **indulge** their whims with a **remarkable** degree of freedom. By embracing a more innocent **mindset**, they can also explore creative interests with a child's sense of wonder. At the same time, with few financial or family responsibilities, people can spend more time learning about themselves. As
35 psychologist Jeffrey Arnett puts it, kidults can "work on becoming the kind of person they want to be."

The question is, will they take advantage of the opportunity? There's a risk that the longer people put off growing up, the harder it will eventually be. By focusing on material goods, entertainment, and short-term pursuits,
40 kidults may **ignore** their intellectual and emotional development. James Cote, a sociologist, has noted that people are not being pressured to mature. That can lead to trouble forming adult relationships and
45 social skills. There's also the danger that kidults, accustomed to having their meals cooked and clothes washed for them, may never learn to take care of themselves.

The average age of video game players is 29 years old.

Kidults are often compared to Peter Pan, a fictional character who flies
50 around, lives in Neverland, and never grows up. Though we can't stop time, the maturation process does seem to be slowing down. As daily life becomes more complex, it's taking people longer to learn to live independently, so the traditional idea that adulthood starts at 18 may soon be a thing of the past. That holds true for countries as diverse as Japan, Germany, and Canada.
55 So, to all those adults with Hello Kitty T-shirts and toy robots, **take heart**. You've got plenty of company.

---

[31] whim – something done without much thought or consideration
[37] take advantage of – make the most of
[38] put off – delay
[39] pursuit – interest; goal
[40] intellectual – related to the mind (ex: interests, ideas, thought processes)

Choose the best answer.

.... **Main Idea**

    1. (   ) What is the main idea?
        A. Many adults have interests that are often associated with childhood.
        B. Companies have found numerous ways to market to kidults.
        C. More and more adult Americans are living with their parents.
        D. Nobody wants to accept responsibility or work hard.

.... **Detail**

    2. (   ) Who suggested that kidults have an opportunity for self-improvement?
        A. Christopher Noxon   B. James Cote
        C. Cyndi Lauper   D. Jeffrey Arnett

.... **Vocabulary**

    3. (   ) In line 31, what does "embracing" mean?
        A. creating   B. welcoming
        C. challenging   D. escaping

.... **Analysis**

    4. (   ) According to the article, what do kidults risk?
        A. Running out of things to purchase
        B. Having problems developing social skills
        C. Not learning how to avoid responsibility
        D. Being heavily pressured to mature

    5. (   ) Why are people taking longer to learn to live independently?
        A. Parents don't want their children to move out.
        B. The world is full of impossible challenges.
        C. Daily life is becoming more complicated.
        D. Traditions are changing in very few countries.

Short Answers   **Answer each question based on the article.**

    1. In 2005, what was the average marriage age in Ireland?

       _____

    2. How have companies benefited from the kidult trend?

       _____

    3. What does James Cote suggest about the way people are growing up?

       _____

Vocabulary Building

A **Choose the answer that means the same as the word or phrase in italics.**

1. When a big movie is released, merchandisers such as toy makers and stationery suppliers try to *cash in on* the opportunity.
   A. pay attention to   B. profit from   C. learn about

2. Most guests *opt* to pay a bit more for the buffet breakfast.
   A. choose   B. forget   C. oppose

3. One *ramification* of promoting Lucy will be upsetting Maurice, who thinks he deserves the job.
   A. result   B. reason   C. remark

4. It's hard to understand the *mindset* of people who spend too much on clothes and then complain about credit card bills.
   A. finances   B. majority   C. attitude

5. *Stay put* while I get the car from the parking garage.
   A. Stay away   B. Remain here   C. Clean up

B **Complete each sentence with the best word or phrase. Remember to use the correct word form.**

take heart   coin a term   pros and cons   mature   disposable income

1. We should probably call people who think all the time "thinkaholics," to _____.

2. A lot of teenagers get part-time jobs to increase their _____.

3. Vacationers to Greece can _____, since there are still some fantastic travel deals available.

4. Julia, who just turned eight, is very _____ for her age. She never complains or causes trouble.

5. Writing down the _____ can help you make a decision.

C **Circle the correct form of each word.**

1. Sometimes, (ignore/ignoring) a problem is the easiest way to deal with it.

2. As an (indulgence/indulge), we have a big ice cream sundae once a month.

3. During the thunderstorm, the pilot worked hard to keep the aircraft as (steady/steadily) as possible.

4. The boxes fell out of the back of the truck as it sped down the highway. (Remarkable/Remarkably), none of the contents were damaged.

5. Mr. Griffin is known for being (blunt/bluntly), but fair, with his employees.

Part 2: Focus Areas

Focus on Language

Word Parts

Study the word parts in the chart. Then, read the following pairs of sentences. Circle if the second sentence is true or false.

Word Part	Meaning	Examples
neg-	no	negate, negativity
-cent-	hundred	centennial, percent
-ism	state; quality	racism, capitalism

1. Dennis responded negatively to the charge that he often arrived late.
   Dennis admitted he had trouble arriving on time. (True / False)

2. The award is only given out once per century.
   Every ten years, someone receives the honor. (True / False)

3. Mr. Kim showed real heroism by pulling a child from the burning building.
   Mr. Kim's actions were selfless and praiseworthy. (True / False)

Grammar — *Passive Form of the Present Progressive*

This structure expresses an ongoing effort to get someone to do something (or not). First, the person (or group, company, etc.) is stated. That's followed by the action being taken. Finally, the goal is stated.

Structure: **s + be (+ not) + being + pp + infinitive**

Ex: Frida is being pressured to study harder for her nursing license.

Ex: Companies aren't being asked to do enough to help the environment.

Complete each sentence using the present progressive + pp. Use the verb in parentheses.

1. A: I hear Ron's parents really want him to become a doctor.
   B: Yes, he _____ (encourage) to study medicine.

2. A: The newspaper said the suspects' lawyers want them to stay silent.
   B: Right, they _____ (advise) to say as little as possible.

3. A: Employees have to work on holidays, right?
   B: No, employees _____ (force) to work on holidays.

58

Talk About It   **Discuss these questions in small groups.**

1. Should people live with their parents as long as they like, or should they leave their parents' home after finishing school?

2. What are the biggest differences between being an adult today and being an adult 50 years ago?

3. In your opinion, is there any harm in being a kidult? Are they just adults enjoying life, or are they avoiding growing up?

Write About It

Question: Some scholars say people are growing up more slowly than before. Others say the opposite is true. What do you think? Give two reasons to support your opinion. Prepare by writing notes on the lines below. The first few words of the paragraph are written to help you get started.

Opinion: _____

Reason 1: _____

Reason 2: _____

It seems to me that people are growing up _____

_____

_____

_____

_____

_____

_____

_____

_____

Listening   **Listen to the message. Then, answer the following questions.**

Track
23

1. ( ) What is the woman's likely occupation?
     (A) Home inspector
     (B) Travel agent
     (C) Tour guide
     (D) City official

2. ( ) What is the disadvantage of the suburban rental?
     (A) The price
     (B) The size
     (C) The location
     (D) The view

3. ( ) What is Alex asked to do?
     (A) Travel to Chicago
     (B) Send an e-mail
     (C) Return a phone call
     (D) Purchase an apartment

Reading   **Choose the correct word(s) to fill in each blank.**

Economist Ali Kapur has coined a new term: Dollarism. (__1__) Dr. Kapur's analysis, companies have mastered the art of pricing entertainment items like video games and movie tickets. The (__2__) is to lure as large a percentage of consumers' disposable income as possible. Companies know people will think long and hard about expensive purchases like TV sets. Yet they're far more likely to indulge themselves on items that represent a small percentage of their salaries. That's the concept of dollarism – to encourage (__3__) small purchases which, over time, add up to a substantial amount of money. There is one drawback. For such a strategy to work, the products must appeal to a large number of consumers.

1. ( ) (A) In addition to   (B) Absent from
     (C) According to   (D) Aimed at

2. ( ) (A) representative   (B) objective
     (C) elective   (D) plaintive

3. ( ) (A) relatively   (B) relativity
     (C) relative   (D) relatives

Supplementary Reading - *Japan's Freeters* Track 24

Japan's version of kidults, known as "freeters," has been widely publicized for decades. The term comes from a combination of the English word "free" and the German word for laborer – "arbeiter." The reference to work is not a coincidence. In the late 1980s, at the height of Japan's bubble economy, a growing number of young people chose not to follow traditional career paths after graduating from high school or university. Instead, they opted for a chance to pursue their dreams. Dubbed "freeters," they lived with their parents and took part-time or short-term jobs for disposable income.

In the early years of the phenomenon, freeters were somewhat idealized for having the conviction to live outside of the "lifetime employment" system. Yet during the long 1990s recession, an increasing number of people adopted a freeter lifestyle out of necessity. The situation worsened further in the 2000s when firms started hiring more workers on a contract basis. In a sense, the freeter phenomenon has paralleled general changes in Japan's culture and economy.

Of the numerous surveys carried out to understand the trend, one in the early 2000s examined how freeters saw themselves. Researchers found that for those who enjoyed the lifestyle, the most common reason (36%) was because of the free time it provided. Another popular response (24%) was that it was important to follow one's dreams. Of those freeters who were unhappy with their situations, 26% said it was because of the instability. Tellingly, 23% of those surveyed said they were looking for a full-time job.

Read each sentence. Circle if it is true (T) or false (F).

1. The freeter phenomenon has been well known since 1980.   T / F
2. During the "bubble economy," freeters were uninterested in lifetime   T / F
   employment.
3. Japan's employment trends have influenced the freeter trend.   T / F
4. In the survey, just over one-fourth of freeters who said they were   T / F
   unhappy disliked the instability.
5. A majority of freeters surveyed would prefer a traditional career.   T / F

7 Nature

Genetically Modified Food

Thanks to advances in genetic engineering, we can make a variety of changes to a food crop's DNA. The practice became widespread in the 1990s and has continued to grow ever since. Genetically modified food crops provide several advantages; however, there is strong opposition to the practice.

Pre-Reading Questions Discuss these questions in pairs.

1. Why would food producers want to modify a crop's genes?

2. Some people are opposed to this practice. Why do you think that is?

3. How do you feel about eating genetically modified food? Is it safe?

Vocabulary Warmup Track 25

A Listen to the unit's target vocabulary. Then, write the letter of the correct word or phrase next to each definition.

a. allergic	f. genetics	k. monopoly
b. biotech	g. harsh	l. organism
c. boost	h. justification	m. patent
d. devoted to	i. legitimate	n. pesticide
e. drought	j. manipulate	o. unforeseen

___ 1. reasoning behind an action

___ 2. long period without rainfall

___ 3. a living being

___ 4. chemical which kills harmful insects

___ 5. committed to

___ 6. not predicted or anticipated

___ 7. valid; reasonable

___ 8. difficult; severe

___ 9. increase; assist

___ 10. total control over an industry

B Complete each sentence with a target word or phrase. Remember to use the correct word form.

1. Governments can _____ a currency by buying or selling it on the open market.

2. Our knowledge of _____ allows us to alter the DNA of plants, animals, and even people.

3. After a number of years, the _____ on a drug expires, allowing other companies to produce and sell it.

4. _____ companies invest huge amounts of money developing new seeds and other agricultural products.

5. People who are _____ to certain foods need to be careful not to eat them.

Part 1: Reading and Vocabulary Building

1 Scientific advances have given us an unprecedented level of control over nature. In medicine, **genetics** is unlocking the secrets of diseases, leading to a golden age of healing. Likewise, in agriculture, we can **manipulate** a plant's genome, changing its DNA for a variety of purposes. Supporters say
5 genetically modified (GM) crops have the potential to end world hunger. Opponents say the practice is dangerous to people and the environment.

Through selective breeding, farmers have directed natural selection for thousands of years. Yet it's a slow process. The game changed completely in the late 20th century. In 1973, scientists invented "recombinant DNA
10 technology," a technique allowing a single gene from one **organism** to be inserted into another. Then, in 1976, the first **biotech** company was founded. The next year, a technique was created to inject individual genes into a plant. Scientists soon put the practice to work, providing farmers with a variety of GM seeds.

15 In 1996, 4.3 million acres were **devoted to** GM crops. By 2006, that had grown to 252 million acres in more than 20 countries, including the USA, Brazil, and China. Soybeans, potatoes, and tomatoes are among the many crops whose genomes have been altered. One of the most commonly inserted genes is BT, which was patented by biotech giant Monsanto. A bacterium that causes
20 plants to produce a natural insecticide, BT is used in crops like corn, cotton, and apples.

Creating pest-resistant plants is one of the main **justifications** for modifying crops, since it reduces the need for chemical **pesticides**. Crops can also be engineered to be disease or herbicide resistant, or they can be altered to **boost**
25 their nutritional levels. For instance, GM crops which produce nutrients like iron and vitamin A can help fight malnutrition in impoverished countries. GM crops which are **drought** resistant are able to survive in **harsh** climates,

---

¹ unprecedented – never before seen or done
⁴ genome – an organism's complete set of genes
⁷ natural selection – the evolution of animals through the prospering of
         stronger, well-adapted members of the species
¹⁹ patent – register an original idea, product, etc., to protect the copyright
²⁴ herbicide – poison designed to kill weeds and other harmful plants

allowing poor countries to use land that was previously non-arable.

Despite these advantages, critics say GM crops aren't worth it. First, there are
environmental risks. It has been shown that the new genes in GM foods can
cross over to non-modified crops or wild plants. This "outcrossing" could
have **unforeseen** consequences for the affected species. Also, there's concern
that pesticide-resistant plants will lead to the growth of "super pests" which
will be difficult to stop. A similar argument points to the possible growth of
"super weeds" in response to herbicide-resistant crops.

Opponents are also concerned about potential risks to people. If a gene from
an allergen such as peanuts is added to a crop, and then eaten by someone
who is **allergic** to peanuts, the consequences
could be severe. What's more, groups like
Greenpeace note that no long-term studies
on the effects of eating GM foods have been
carried out. There's also concern that biotech
companies, by controlling **patents** over the
seeds they develop, could hold a **monopoly**
over our food supply. The high price of GM
seeds could be devastating to farmers in poor
countries.

Vocal protests against GM foods have influenced legislation in several countries.

It's a complex debate, with **legitimate** arguments on both sides. To ease
public fears, the WHO points out that no GM foods on the market have
been shown to pose a health risk. Measures can also be taken to limit the
risk of problems like outcrossing. Still, opposition to GM foods remains
fierce, particularly in Europe, which has strict laws regulating their sale and
labeling. Nevertheless, considering the size of the biotech industry ($73.5
billion in 2007), it's likely that the use of technology to manipulate crops will
continue to grow. As that happens, agribusinesses will continue to face tough
questions and challenges.

28 non-arable – unable to be used as farmland (since crops will not grow there)
37 allergen – something that causes an allergic reaction in people
46 devastating – extremely harmful
48 ease – lessen
49 WHO – World Health Organization
55 agribusiness – firm involved in an agricultural industry

Choose the best answer.

.........**Main Idea**

1. (   ) What is the main idea?
   A. Despite the potential benefits of GM foods, they face serious opposition.
   B. Outcrossing involves a gene from one species jumping over to another.
   C. BT is a bacterium inserted into the DNA of crops like soybeans.
   D. People enjoy nutritious foods that are grown with few chemicals.

.........**Detail**

2. (   ) When did scientists learn to place individual genes into a plant's genome?
   A. 1973   B. 1976
   C. 1977   D. 2007

.........**Vocabulary**

3. (   ) In line 52, what does "regulating" mean?
   A. preventing   B. upholding
   C. protesting   D. governing

.........**Analysis**

4. (   ) According to the article, why are some groups opposed to GM foods?
   A. We still don't know how GM foods may affect us over the long run.
   B. It's impossible to keep allergens like peanuts out of GM foods.
   C. Studies by the WHO have revealed the health risks of GM foods.
   D. GM foods could have a negative effect on companies like Monsanto.

5. (   ) Which of the following is NOT a suggested benefit of GM foods?
   A. A reduced need for chemical pesticides
   B. The ability of crops to survive droughts
   C. The production of nutrient-rich foods
   D. Cost savings on seeds for poor farmers

Short Answers   **Answer each question based on the article.**

1. How long have farmers been practicing selective breeding?

_____

2. What is the advantage of adding BT to a plant's genome?

_____

3. How much was the biotech industry worth in 2007?

_____

Vocabulary Building

A **Choose the answer that means the same as the word or phrase in italics.**

1. Receiving orders from several large corporations was an *unforeseen*, yet well-appreciated outcome.
   A. unplanned   B. unlikely   C. unaffected

2. Using a high-grade motor oil can *boost* your performance by 10 percent.
   A. increase   B. extend   C. rival

3. What *justification* can they have for making home repairs at 3:00 AM?
   A. referral   B. reasoning   C. negotiation

4. The scientist has been accused of *manipulating* his results to achieve a preferred outcome.
   A. creating   B. altering   C. securing

5. Businesses which stay *devoted to* their ideals have strong customer bases.
   A. aware of   B. faithful to   C. separated from

B **Complete each sentence with the best word. Remember to use the correct word form.**

genetics	pesticide	biotech	drought	organism

1. Strict laws limit the amount of _____ you can use on a crop.

2. The Earth is so rich with life that there are living _____ everywhere, even in barren places.

3. Several _____ companies are developing machines with organic components.

4. If the _____ lasts any longer, they'll have to restrict the supply of water to homes and businesses.

5. Some people think _____ can explain our behavior. Others say environmental factors are key. And others say it's a bit of both.

C **Circle the correct form of each word.**

1. The smell coming from the lake is a (legitimate/legitimately) concern.

2. We're worried that the supermarket chain will (monopoly/monopolize) the industry by buying all of its competitors.

3. If you have any (allergies/allergic), please write them down on the form.

4. The recruit complained about being treated (harsh/harshly) by his superior.

5. We're in the process of obtaining a (patent/patented) for our engine design.

Part 2: Focus Areas

Focus on Language

Word Parts

Study the word parts in the chart. Then, read the following pairs of sentences. Circle if the second sentence is true or false.

Word Part	Meaning	Examples
op-	against	oppress, oppose
-techn(o)-	skill	technological, technician
-cide	killing	homicide, genocide

1. Sheryl is a firm opponent of the proposed land reclamation project.
   Sheryl has not yet made up her mind about the project. (True / False)

2. A flying house is a fantastic idea, but it isn't technologically possible.
   Turning the concept into reality isn't feasible. (True / False)

3. The nation was shocked by the patricide case involving a wealthy family.
   The murder of the rich father surprised everyone. (True / False)

Grammar *Likewise vs. Likely*

These two terms are easily confused. *Likewise*, which is an adverb, means "also" or "similarly." *Likely*, which is also an adverb, means "with a good possibility of happening."

Ex: Greta is from northern England. Likewise, Rasheem is from the same part of the country.

Ex: The weather report said rain is likely, so bring your umbrella.

Complete each sentence with *likewise* or *likely*.

1. If you're _____ to be late, please let me know in advance.

2. We're going to take a bus into town. John, _____, will go by bus.

3. The size of the suitcase isn't _____ to be a problem.

4. We can ship it by airmail, but it will _____ cost $50 or more.

5. Karen is very shy. _____, her sister tends to keep to herself.

68

Talk About It   Discuss these questions in small groups.

1. Producing GM foods involves risks and rewards. Are the rewards worth it, or are the risks too great?

2. If a food product contains genetically modified food, should the producer be required to say so on the packaging?

3. GM foods are part of a bigger issue: people directing the course of nature. Is this something we're ready for, or do we need to slow down?

Write About It

Question: GM seeds are expensive. Should manufacturers be required to sell them at a discount to poor farmers? Give two reasons to support your opinion. Prepare by writing notes on the lines below. The first few words of the paragraph are written to help you get started.

Opinion: _____

Reason 1: _____

Reason 2: _____

In terms of discounts for GM seeds, I feel _____

_____

_____

_____

_____

_____

_____

_____

Listening

Listen to the conversation. Then, answer the following questions.

Track 27

1. (   ) What is the man's likely occupation?
   (A) Nutritionist   (B) Researcher
   (C) Gardener   (D) Grocer

2. (   ) What does the woman suggest about her cucumbers?
   (A) They're hard to grow.
   (B) They're healthier than her squash.
   (C) They're growing well.
   (D) They're sicker than her carrots.

3. (   ) How does the woman feel about pesticides?
   (A) She's open to using them.   (B) She thinks they're immoral.
   (C) She can't afford them.   (D) She'd prefer another solution.

Reading

Read the information. Then, answer the following questions.

The theme of the 7th annual Canadian Biotech Conference is "GM Issues: Innovation and Responsibility." These questions will be addressed:

1. From a research perspective, what is the state of the industry? What are the year's most important breakthroughs?
2. Have we done an adequate job educating the public on the benefits of GM foods? Or are we losing the public relations fight?
3. How can we improve public/private partnerships to encourage government investment and streamline the patent approval process?
4. Should we increase the size of the Developing Country Assistance Program to provide additional seeds to poor countries?

Dr. Fred Marshall, the director of Bioforce's Genetics Lab, will deliver the plenary speech. He'll share his perspective on recent advances in the field.

1. (   ) What area of potential concern will the conference address?
   (A) Seed quality   (B) Research budgets
   (C) Public perception   (D) Environmental protests

2. (   ) What can be inferred about participating biotech firms?
   (A) They rarely collaborate with Bioforce's Genetics Lab.
   (B) They are unwilling to lower prices for poor farmers.
   (C) They resist interacting with government agencies.
   (D) They donate a certain quantity of their products.

3. (   ) Of the four question areas, which does Dr. Marshall's speech cover?
   (A) Question 1   (B) Question 2
   (C) Question 3   (D) Question 4

Supplementary Reading - *Europe vs. GM Foods*   Track 28

Europe has long been at the forefront of the fight against GM foods. Opposition has been strong since the 1990s, a decade which saw a series of food scares including the near panic over mad cow disease. GM foods were sold in the UK as early as 1996, when a form of engineered tomato was marketed. Yet shortly thereafter, a study in Scotland suggested that certain GM products caused health problems in rats.

As the 20th century neared its close, the study contributed to a deafening public uproar, resulting in a 1999 moratorium on GM products. A number of strict labeling laws were also enacted. For instance, food products containing more than 1% of GM content had to be labeled as such. The

moratorium was lifted in 2004, yet a number of countries, including Austria and Hungary, have maintained outright bans on the cultivation of certain GM crops. Their citizens are still concerned about outcrossing as well as potential negative effects of GM foods on humans.

In recent years, the EU has come under considerable pressure to relax its restrictions. Major biotech companies such as Monsanto (USA) and Bayer (Germany) have the backing of the World Trade Organization and powerful countries like the USA and Canada. However, several EU nations have refused to give in and have even intensified their opposition. For instance, in 2009, Germany became the sixth EU member to ban the growth of a type of GM maize. In Europe at least, the controversy over non-natural foods isn't likely to end anytime soon.

Read each sentence. Circle if it is true (T) or false (F).

1. The Scottish study was conducted before GM tomatoes went on sale in the UK.   T / F

2. The EU moratorium on GM foods lasted less than a decade.   T / F

3. In Europe, if a packaged food product is 90% GM-free, it doesn't need a special label.   T / F

4. The USA would like to see Europe open its markets to GM foods.   T / F

5. In 2009, Germany ended its long-standing opposition to GM crops.   T / F

8 Entertainment

Empires of the Stars

These days, celebrities are selling more than CDs and movie tickets. They're using their fame to grow their fortunes through a variety of business ventures. Many endorse products. Others lend their names to consumer goods. A few even found companies, which can grow into industry leaders.

Pre-Reading Questions Discuss these questions in pairs.

1. What types of products are often endorsed by celebrities?

2. Can you think of any celebrities who have started their own product lines?

3. What does it take for a star's business ventures to be successful?

Vocabulary Warmup Track 29

A **Listen to the unit's target vocabulary. Then, write the letter of the correct word or phrase next to each definition.**

a. boast	f. flourish	k. lucrative
b. connoisseur	g. get into the act	l. savvy
c. discipline	h. infant	m. transform
d. endorsement	i. juggernaut	n. walk of life
e. fleeting	j. leverage	o. woo

___ 1. completely change

___ 2. win over

___ 3. support; backing

___ 4. an expert

___ 5. very young baby

___ 6. lasting a short period of time

___ 7. self-control

___ 8. participate

___ 9. thrive; succeed

___ 10. very powerful person, business, etc.

B **Complete each sentence with a target word or phrase. Remember to use the correct word form.**

1. Well-known chefs can _____ their fame to work at any restaurant they want.

2. With 30 years of experience in the field, Mr. Simmons has more wisdom and business _____ than anyone I know.

3. Places like Disneyland attract visitors from all _____, including some famous and powerful people.

4. Despite the economic downturn, the hotel _____ a 12% rise in profits last year.

5. The family doesn't need its business to be too _____. As long as it earns enough to cover costs, they'll be happy.

Part 1: Reading and Vocabulary Building

1   In the world of celebrity, fame is **fleeting**. The majority of stars shine and
fade in a few short years. However, a small number are able to **leverage**
their fame and wealth, turning themselves into extremely successful brands.
Often possessing a high degree of marketing **savvy**, these actors, singers, and

5   athletes have branched into the clothing, perfume, and restaurant industries,
to name a few. In the words of *Fortune* magazine, "today's elite celebrities
are no longer just building wealth, they're building empires."

For decades, athletes and other celebrities have used their star power
to land **endorsement** deals. They have appeared in commercials, print

10 advertisements, and on the packaging of
everything from deodorant to canned coffee.
In the 1980s, these deals became very **lucrative**.
Michael Jordan was one of the first to use his
business savvy (and unparalleled star power)

15 to secure excellent terms from partners like
Nike. He still receives a percentage of the
revenues for every pair of Air Jordan shoes
sold. Many other athletes, such as Ichiro Suzuki

*A singer's popularity makes it easy for
him or her to sell branded products.*

(Japan), LeBron James (USA), and Maria Sharapova (Russia) have inked

20 endorsement deals with a wide range of companies.

The next step for many celebrities is lending their names to lifestyle
products. Stars from many **walks of life**, including Celine Dion and David
Beckham, have backed fragrances. Jennifer Lopez has a number of perfumes
which bring in annual sales topping $100 million. Celebrities have also done

25 well with signature clothing brands. Arnold Palmer, the legendary golfer,
was one of the first to do so. He's been followed by the likes of Jackie Chan
and the Olsen twins (Mary-Kate and Ashley). The American actresses,
famous since they were **infants**, founded a company when they were eight

---

⁴ possess – have
⁶ to name a few – among others
⁶ elite – top; leading
¹⁴ unparalleled – unmatched; unequaled
²⁵ signature brand – a brand named after a person

years old! More than a decade later, sales of their cosmetics, clothing, and
other lifestyle products continue to **flourish**.

The restaurant business has also been a natural fit for celebrity entrepreneurs.
Stars can use their connections in the entertainment industry to generate
publicity for a restaurant, and through personal appearances, they can
woo the clientele. Robert De Niro is one of the best-known **connoisseurs**.
Partnering with the famous chef Nobu Matsuhisa, he started a chain of sushi
restaurants that now **boasts** 25 locations in 11 countries. Jackie Chan has also
gotten into the act, with a chain of cafés in Singapore, the Philippines, and
Malaysia.

Some celebrities do a little bit of everything, **transforming** their brands into
juggernaut firms. One such success story is Tony Hawk, who has been the
world's most famous skateboarder since the 1980s. Now, his name is on
everything from video games to roller coasters. What's more, through Tony
Hawk Inc., he creates sports-related films and puts on live events featuring
skateboarders and other "extreme sports" athletes.

Sean Combs (known as Diddy, among other names), has been similarly busy
(and successful). The hip-hop singer has produced music through his own
record label – Bad Boy Entertainment. On top of that, his clothing company,
Sean John Clothing, has yearly sales surpassing $500 million. But Combs isn't
just making money. His clothing designs have been widely praised, earning
him the Menswear Designer of the Year award from the Council of Fashion
Designers of America.

Of course, things don't always work out the way stars plan. Britney Spears'
restaurant was unsuccessful. And, despite the backing of superstars like
Arnold Schwarzenegger and Bruce Willis, the Planet Hollywood chain of
restaurants went bankrupt twice. Thus, just having money and fame aren't
enough. To be successful, stars also need a good business model, strong
marketing instincts, and solid financial **discipline**.

---

[31] entrepreneur – person who starts a company or backs other business opportunities
[34] clientele – customer base
[43] put on – direct; produce
[44] extreme sports – a thrilling class of sports including snowboarding, bike racing, etc.
[48] surpass – go beyond
[57] instinct – natural sense of what to do

.... **Main Idea**

1. ( ) What is the main idea?
   A. Athletes get more endorsement deals than singers.
   B. Fragrances are one of the most profitable types of lifestyle products.
   C. Some stars have used their business savvy to become more wealthy.
   D. Fame does not last long for a majority of celebrities.

.... **Detail**

2. ( ) Who did Robert De Niro work with to open a chain of restaurants?
   A. Jackie Chan   B. Michael Jordan
   C. Nobu Matsuhisa   D. Jennifer Lopez

.... **Vocabulary**

3. ( ) In line 19, what does "inked" mean?
   A. played   B. referred
   C. signed   D. sponsored

.... **Analysis**

4. ( ) What do Arnold Palmer and Ashley Olsen have in common?
   A. They're both well-known athletes who sell lifestyle products.
   B. Arnold and Ashley both have twin siblings.
   C. The two of them were famous as children.
   D. Both of them have done well through their own clothing lines.

5. ( ) What can be inferred about Sean Combs?
   A. He is taken seriously as a clothing designer.
   B. He earns more from music sales than clothing sales.
   C. He was the first singer to start a clothing line.
   D. He runs the Council of Fashion Designers of America.

Short Answers   Answer each question based on the article.

1. How does Michael Jordan make money from the sale of Air Jordan shoes?

   _____

2. Which countries feature a Jackie Chan café?

   _____

3. What are three products or business activities that Tony Hawk is involved with?

   _____

Vocabulary Building

A Choose the answer that means the same as the word or phrase in italics.

1. On International Student Day, one way to *get into the act* is by volunteering at the information booth.
   A. overcome   B. participate   C. translate

2. Believe it or not, small food stalls in good locations can be very *lucrative*.
   A. crowded   B. popular   C. rewarding

3. If you have a skill that companies need, it gives you *leverage* in the job market.
   A. power   B. experience   C. reputation

4. Margaret is a *connoisseur* who can tell you all about 100 kinds of cheese.
   A. manufacturer   B. exporter   C. expert

5. IBM is a *juggernaut* in the computer industry.
   A. powerhouse   B. competitor   C. founder

B Complete each sentence with the best word or phrase. Remember to use the correct word form.

woo	discipline	boast	walk of life	savvy

1. When you work from home, you need _____, a good work ethic, and plenty of motivation.

2. As a small amusement park, we can't _____ of Disney-like attendance levels, but we do pretty well.

3. Some people are born with a degree of business _____. Others acquire it through years of experience.

4. During anniversary sales, department stores try to _____ potential customers by promising steep discounts.

5. The jazz band has fans from many _____, including professors, doctors, and scientists.

C Circle the correct form of each word.

1. A (flourish/flourishing) community of eagles lives on the mountainside.

2. Redeveloping the pier has (transformed/transforming) the district into one of the city's nicest areas.

3. People running for public office appreciate the (endorse/endorsement) of business and community leaders.

4. Now 28, Eileen has lived in the same house since (infant/infancy).

5. Outside the theater, I caught a (fleeting/fleetingly) glimpse of Brad Pitt!

Part 2: Focus Areas

Focus on Language

Word Parts

Study the word parts in the chart. Then, read the following pairs of sentences. Circle if the second sentence is true or false.

Word Part	Meaning	Examples
super-	above; beyond	supernatural, superficial
-nat-	birth	native, cognate
-ary	related to	momentary, solitary

1. Critics say George Clooney delivered a superior performance in the film.
   Clooney's effort in the movie was widely criticized. (True / False)

2. The chameleon has an innate ability to change colors.
   The animal learns the skill long after it's born. (True / False)

3. Sam's dentist told him the numbness in his mouth would be temporary.
   The numbness was only expected to last a short while. (True / False)

Grammar *Appositives*

Appositives are nouns or noun phrases which provide more information about another noun. An appositive usually follows the noun which it modifies. However, it can also appear before the noun.

Ex: Lance, an outstanding engineer, is redesigning our power supply.

Ex: One of the fastest cars you can buy, a Ferrari is a masterpiece of precision.

Combine the two sentences into one sentence by using an appositive.

1. That's a Commodore Vic-20. It's one of the earliest personal computers.

   _____

2. Stephanie will arrive on Monday. She's the friend I told you about.

   _____

3. Gold has many uses and is in demand worldwide. It's a precious metal.

   _____

Talk About It   Discuss these questions in small groups.

1. It's difficult for celebrities to hold onto their star power for more than a few years. Why is that?

2. To get big endorsement deals, stars must carefully maintain a positive public image. How easy or difficult is it for them to keep that up?

3. Would you pay more to eat at a celebrity restaurant if you had the chance to see one of your favorite stars there? Why or why not?

Write About It

Question: Many young people see celebrities as role models. Is that a good or bad idea? Give two reasons to support your opinion. Prepare by writing notes on the lines below. The first few words of the paragraph are written to help you get started.

Opinion: _____

Reason 1: _____

Reason 2: _____

In my opinion, celebrities are _____

_____

_____

_____

_____

_____

_____

_____

_____

Listening **Listen to the report. Then, answer the following questions.**

Track
31

1. (   ) What is the main topic of the report?
     (A) A newly opened mine
     (B) The future of precious metals
     (C) The Chilean economy
     (D) A corporate takeover

2. (   ) What is considered a key motivator for Tecton?
     (A) Expanding their aluminum portfolio
     (B) Acquiring a copper mine
     (C) Cornering the coal market
     (D) Adding to their silver and gold holdings

3. (   ) What must be obtained before any deal can go through?
     (A) Board approval
     (B) Stockholder agreement
     (C) Investor support
     (D) Government consent

Reading **Choose the correct word(s) to fill in each blank.**

As celebrities appear and disappear at an ever-quickening rate, fame is more fleeting than ever. It's no wonder stars (and their managers) work (___1___) aggressively to capitalize on their time in the public eye. They often work as quickly as possible to leverage their fame and secure their financial future. Star Connection, a consulting firm which (___2___) in celebrity endorsements, can help stars with the process. With years of experience dealing with corporate sponsors, they're experts at "image matching" – that is, bringing together actors, actresses, and singers with companies looking to attract a target demographic. Yet stars need to be careful not to (___3___) themselves too aggressively or accept too many endorsements, since that can saturate their image and weaken their popularity.

1. (   ) (A) for   (B) so
      (C) to   (D) on

2. (   ) (A) specializes   (B) to specialize
      (C) specializing   (D) specialize

3. (   ) (A) sponsor   (B) attract
      (C) protect   (D) market

Supplementary Reading - *Newman's Own* Track 32

In terms of celebrity food labels, few can match the popularity of Newman's Own. The firm was started in 1982 by film legend Paul Newman, the star of movies like *Cool Hand Luke* and *The Sting*. "Old blue eyes," as he was affectionately known, enjoyed making, bottling, and giving away salad dressing. The actor thought it might be fun to sell the dressing to the general public, so he founded Newman's Own with just the one product. Little did he suspect that millions of bottles would sell in the first two years!

Over the decades, the firm's product line, which features Paul Newman's image on the packaging, has grown to include fruit juice, pasta sauce, frozen pizza, and more. The company's first guiding principle is its products are all-natural, with no added preservatives. The concept, though widespread now, was progressive in the  early 1980s. The healthy, yet tasty goods made by Newman's Own are sold in more than a dozen countries, from the USA to Iceland to Singapore.

Charity is another guiding principle of the company, which gives away all of its profits through the Newman's Own Foundation. From 1982 to 2009, some $280 million went to disaster relief, poverty fighting efforts, clean water initiatives, and many other causes. One of the flagship programs is a network of Hole in the Wall Camps. These free camps provide fun and encouraging programs for children with serious illnesses. They've been set up in 39 countries and have brought hope and happiness to more than 100,000 kids.

Read each sentence. Circle if it is true (T) or false (F).

1. Paul Newman started Newman's Own as a way to become famous.   T / F
2. Before founding the company, Paul Newman knew his salad dressing would be popular.   T / F
3. The Newman's Own product line includes food, drinks, and sauces.   T / F
4. The firm started giving money to charity in 2009.   T / F
5. Hole in the Wall Camps have donated nearly $300 million worldwide.   T / F

9 Space

Destination: Mars

In recent years, amazing discoveries about other planets, including Mars, have rekindled public interest in space exploration. So far, every mission to Mars has used unmanned craft and robotic vehicles. Though plans are being developed to send people to Mars, such a mission will be very challenging.

Pre-Reading Questions   Discuss these questions in pairs.

1. Do you follow the news about Mars or any other space programs? If so, what interesting news have you heard recently?

2. What would be challenging about traveling to Mars?

3. If you had the chance, would you like to go to Mars? Why or why not?

Vocabulary Warmup Track 33

A Listen to the unit's target vocabulary. Then, write the letter of the correct word next to each definition.

a. adequate	f. embark	k. pioneer
b. arise	g. menacing	l. radiation
c. bombard	h. orbit	m. retrieve
d. chamber	i. oxygen	n. revive
e. daunting	j. peer	o. speculation

___ 1. threatening; fierce

___ 2. challenging; formidable

___ 3. guess; uninformed opinion

___ 4. look closely at; stare

___ 5. begin a journey; board a ship

___ 6. room

___ 7. enough; sufficient

___ 8. come up; occur

___ 9. attack; assault

___ 10. revolve around a star, planet, etc.

B Complete each sentence with a target word. Remember to use the correct word form.

1. People who work with _____ must take many safety measures, such as wearing protective clothing.

2. We hope the exhibition will _____ interest in local arts, which are now all but forgotten.

3. If you drop something on the train tracks, ask a rail worker to _____ it for you.

4. Divers carry tanks with enough _____ to stay underwater for an hour or longer.

5. Bill Gates, one of the _____ of the personal computer industry, co-founded Microsoft in 1975.

Part 1: Reading and Vocabulary Building

1   In 1877, Italian astronomer Giovanni Schiaparelli **peered** through the night sky at Mars. His detailed drawings of the surface led to wild **speculation** about the planet. Were there artificial canals criss-crossing the planet? Were **menacing** aliens living there? More than 100 years later, we know
5   considerably more about the dusty red planet. However, the more we learn, the more questions **arise**. To search for answers, while taking our next great leap into space, plans are being drawn up to send people to Mars.

Mars is an excellent candidate for manned exploration. It lies between our planet and the solar system's asteroid belt, making it a great stepping stone
10 for deep space exploration. Also, Mars has incredible surface features, such as the solar system's largest volcano and its deepest canyon. Plus, there's the tantalizing possibility that life once existed on the planet. Mars also has interesting weather patterns, though it gets bitterly cold at night (down to -100°C). Also, massive dust storms caused by powerful winds can be fierce.

15 Space exploration of the rocky planet dates back to the 1960s. The first detailed photographs were provided by Mariner 4, which flew by Mars in 1965. Mariner 9, the first craft to **orbit** the planet, reached Mars in 1971. Another big step was the Viking lander, which touched down on the surface in 1976. A long drought in Mars exploration followed, but it was **revived** by
20 a series of fantastic successes. They included the Mars Odyssey orbiter (2001) and the twin rovers Spirit and Opportunity (2004), which have taken more than 100,000 photographs since landing on the planet.

So far, the work has all been done by unmanned spacecraft and robots. In order to send people to Mars, some **daunting** challenges must first be met.
25 Since it takes six or seven months to travel there, astronauts would have to grow their own food while recycling air and water in a "closed-loop" system. Once on the planet, travelers would need to make use of Martian ice for

---

3   criss-cross – go back and forth across something (often many times)
5   considerably – significantly; very much
9   asteroid belt – region of space between Mars and Jupiter that contains many asteroids
9   stepping stone – something that lets you move on to a farther point
12 tantalizing – creating a lot of interest; very attractive
21 rover – vehicle (usually designed to explore uneven, rough land)

drinking water, **oxygen**, and rocket fuel. Yet the most worrisome problem is invisible. In deep space, several types of **radiation**, such as galactic cosmic
30 rays, would constantly **bombard** the crew. **Adequate** shielding must first be developed to protect them.

A manned mission could take place by 2031. Before then, we'll continue gathering information using robotic orbiters and rovers.
35 Some will focus on the planet's geology and atmosphere, and others will look for signs of organic compounds and microscopic life. One mission under consideration may use a robotic craft and lander to **retrieve** rock, soil,
40 and atmospheric samples and return them to Earth for detailed study.

New rocket and rocket fuel designs may be part of a manned Mars mission.

Important preparation work is also being done on Earth. At the Brookhaven National Laboratory, researchers are studying the heavy ions found in cosmic rays. We need to learn as much as possible about this harmful
45 radiation before people **embark** on long space missions. Also, to study the psychological effects of long-distance space travel, researchers designed the Mars 500 program. The goal is to see how a six-person crew will adjust to living together in a small, sealed **chamber** for 520 days.

There's plenty of support for a manned mission to Mars, including the
50 backing of space **pioneers** like Buzz Aldrin. Unfortunately, there's no escaping one galaxy-sized problem: money. It's increasingly felt that no one country can fly to Mars and back using just its own resources. Thus, in 2009, NASA and the European Space Agency (ESA) began discussing a Mars Exploration Joint Initiative. Perhaps it's fitting that as we plan such an
55 important mission, we do so together – not as separate citizens of any one country, but as common citizens of Earth.

---

29 invisible – unable to be seen
50 backing – support
54 initiative – undertaking; program set up to accomplish a specific goal
54 fitting – appropriate

Reading Comprehension
Choose the best answer.

.........**Main Idea**

1. (　) What is the main idea?
    A. Deep space exploration is full of danger, wonder, and mystery.
    B. It takes at least half a year to fly to Mars.
    C. Interest in Mars was highest in the 1960s.
    D. After many unmanned missions to Mars, people may soon travel there.

.........**Detail**

2. (　) What is the most serious challenge facing a manned journey to Mars?
    A. Blocking radiation　　　B. Creating fuel
    C. Growing food　　　　　D. Recycling air

.........**Vocabulary**

3. (　) In line 13, what does "bitterly" mean?
    A. extremely　　　　　　B. angrily
    C. temporarily　　　　　D. interestingly

.........**Analysis**

4. (　) Which of these events took place first?
    A. A pair of rovers took 100,000 photos of Mars.
    B. A craft began orbiting Mars.
    C. A lander reached the surface of Mars.
    D. A spacecraft flew by Mars.

5. (　) Why may it be necessary for several nations to plan a Mars trip together?
    A. No one country has all the necessary expertise.
    B. The cost of the mission will be very high.
    C. There are insufficient resources on Mars.
    D. NASA and the ESA always work together on missions.

Short Answers
Answer each question based on the article.

1. What are two factors that make Mars a good choice for a manned visit?

   _____

2. How would astronauts get food and water during the journey to Mars?

   _____

3. What does the Mars 500 program seek to understand?

   _____

Vocabulary Building

A **Choose the answer that means the same as the word in italics.**

1. The poster for the horror movie features an image of a *menacing* killer.
   A. frightening   B. gigantic   C. abnormal

2. Visitors can use a telescope to *peer* deep into the canyon.
   A. dive   B. hike   C. stare

3. If any problems *arise* during the experiment, the machine will shut itself off automatically.
   A. revise   B. challenge   C. happen

4. The photographer is complaining that the lighting isn't *adequate*.
   A. professional   B. sufficient   C. contracted

5. In some old castles, rooms contained secret *chambers* for hiding things.
   A. traditions   B. instructions   C. compartments

B **Complete each sentence with the best word. Remember to use the correct word form.**

pioneer	daunting	radiation	oxygen	revive

1. Turning the dump into a park will be a(n) _____ task.

2. With expert skill, the doctor was able to _____ the patient.

3. When _____ leaks from a nuclear power plant, whole communities must be evacuated.

4. Buzz Aldrin, a(n) _____ in manned space flight in the 1960s, has written several books about space.

5. If a person's brain doesn't receive enough _____, he or she will become light-headed.

C **Circle the correct form of each word.**

1. There are hundreds of satellites (orbiting/orbit) the Earth.

2. (Retrieve/Retrieval) of the sunken ship is expected to be carried out later this month.

3. During the Second World War, London went through a prolonged aerial (bombard/bombardment).

4. The police are asking the press to avoid (speculating/speculate) about the murder case until all the evidence has been processed.

5. Before we (embark/embarking), I must remind you to keep your arms and legs inside the vehicle at all times.

Part 2: Focus Areas

Focus on Language

Word Parts

Study the word parts in the chart. Then, read the following pairs of sentences. Circle if the second sentence is true or false.

Word Part	Meaning	Examples
micro-	small	microscope, microphone
-photo-	light	telephoto, photocopy
-some	full of	fearsome, lonesome

1. Tomorrow's microeconomics class will consider the case of a Kenyan firm.
   The class will examine Kenya's role in world diplomacy. (True / False)

2. Some quantum computers use photons to carry out operations.
   Light particles are used by the computers for important functions. (True / False)

3. We have a troublesome neighbor who likes playing loud music at 2:00 AM.
   Getting along with the neighbor is easy. (True / False)

Grammar   *The more...the more*

> This commonly used structure provides an excellent way to discuss how one thing influences another. Plus, it's easy to use, since you only need to add a subject and verb after each instance of *the more*.
>
> Structure: **The more + s + v, the more + s + v**
>
> Ex: The more I learn about Vietnam, the more the country fascinates me.
>
> Ex: The more Flora exercises, the more she feels like a new person.

Combine the sentences into one sentence using *the more...the more.*

1. She has been reading about space. The field interests her more and more.

   _____

2. We're investing in customer service. As a result, our sales are increasing.

   _____

3. We tell our son not to eat candy. He keeps eating more!

   _____

Talk About It — **Discuss these questions in small groups.**

1. A trip to Mars would be very long. How would you spend your time during the six-month journey?

2. A manned mission to Mars would be expensive. Would you mind paying a special tax to help raise money? Why or why not?

3. Some people feel the first person to step on Mars should be from a poor country, as a symbolic gesture of support for the world's poor. Do you agree or disagree? Why?

Write About It

Question: The first manned mission to Mars could be dangerous. Is it worth the risk to the crew? Give two reasons to support your opinion. Prepare by writing notes on the lines below. The first few words of the paragraph are written to help you get started.

Opinion: _____

Reason 1: _____

Reason 2: _____

The way I see it, a manned mission to Mars is

_____

_____

_____

_____

_____

_____

_____

_____

Listening   **Listen to the conversation. Then, answer the following questions.**

Track 35

1. (   ) What kind of product are they selling?
     (A) An energy bar   (B) A beverage
     (C) A vitamin   (D) A dessert

2. (   ) What is the man concerned about?
     (A) The project deadline   (B) The amount of blank space
     (C) The size of the package   (D) The item's nutritional value

3. (   ) What does the woman suggest doing?
     (A) Hiring an actual astronaut
     (B) Developing a new product
     (C) Using space station images
     (D) Researching the moon and Mars

Reading   **Read the article. Then, answer the following questions.**

As we send more satellites and ships into space, the bands of space near our planet are being populated with more and more garbage. Wires, bolts, and other objects orbit the Earth at a very fast rate, posing a risk to satellites, spacecraft, and the International Space Station. In response, a coalition of space agencies wants to send up a robotic vessel to locate and retrieve space debris. Designing the vessel will be a daunting challenge. It will need a strong hull (since it will run the risk of being bombarded by small and large objects), as well as special instruments to grab and store garbage. Scientists on Earth will remotely control the craft, which is expected to cost $200 million.

1. (   ) What is the source of space junk?
     (A) Space-regulating agencies   (B) Items produced in space
     (C) Vessels sent into space   (D) Natural objects from space

2. (   ) The word "rate" in line 3 is closest in meaning to
     (A) cost   (B) degree
     (C) speed   (D) level

3. (   ) What can be inferred about the garbage retrieval vessel?
     (A) The design challenges have all been solved.
     (B) Similar vessels have been used in the past.
     (C) No astronauts will be on board the craft.
     (D) It will cost less to build than other spaceships.

Supplementary Reading - *Colonizing Mars*   Track 36

For some Mars enthusiasts, the idea of traveling to the red planet is just the beginning. They want to see a permanent colony established on our galactic neighbor. These visionaries, including Robert Zubrin, president of the Mars Society and author of *The Case for Mars*, see Mars colonization as the next great step in human exploration.

The first question is technical: how can we survive for months and years so far out in space? The abundance of ice on Mars (and therefore water, oxygen, and hydrogen) could serve many of our basic needs. It's also possible that certain crops could be grown in Martian soil. Far into the

future, it may even be possible to "terraform" Mars, transforming the landscape and atmosphere so they're more suitable for human life.

From a cost standpoint, proponents note that a one-way trip would be far cheaper than a roundtrip mission. The first colonists could bring basic supplies, while other building materials, equipment, and future supplies could be delivered by unmanned spacecraft. Mars also has a rich supply of rare metals, minerals, and other substances which could be mined and shipped to Earth.

Finally, there's a philosophical question: why would we want to settle on a planet that seems so harsh compared to our own? Some point to the ever-shrinking space and resources on Earth. Our planet is filling up, while Mars is empty. Others argue that Mars is the next great frontier, and our thirst for adventure and exploration is as great as it's ever been.

Read each sentence. Circle if it is true (T) or false (F).

1. Robert Zubrin has long been a critic of Mars colonization. T / F
2. Terraforming Mars could easily be accomplished by the first visitors. T / F
3. Transporting colonists to Mars would be cheaper than transporting visitors who intend to return to Earth. T / F
4. There is no economic incentive to colonize Mars. T / F
5. The abundance of available land on Mars could be an important motivator for future colonists. T / F

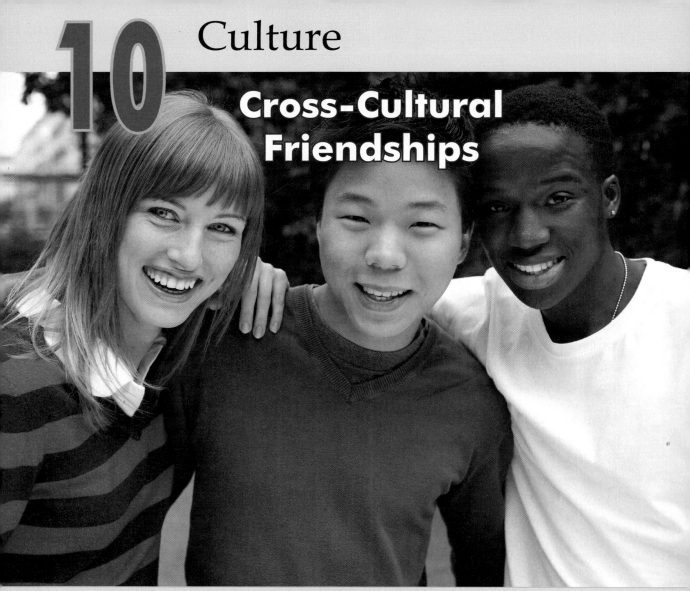

10 Culture

Cross-Cultural Friendships

It's often said that the world is a "global village." What better way to become an active member than by making friends with people from other cultures. Many schools and communities have programs that bring together young people from diverse cultural backgrounds.

Pre-Reading Questions Discuss these questions in pairs.

1. Do you have any friends from other countries or different cultural backgrounds?

2. What are some positive things about making friends with people from other cultures?

3. Many people travel abroad to study. How can local students help international students adjust to life in their host country?

Vocabulary Warmup Track 37

A **Listen to the unit's target vocabulary. Then, write the letter of the correct word or phrase next to each definition.**

a. acclimatize	f. conflict	k. paramount
b. anthropologist	g. dialogue	l. perspective
c. befriend	h. element	m. stereotype
d. broaden (one's) horizons	i. inevitably	n. sympathetic
e. compound	j. introverted	o. vice-versa

___ 1. very shy

___ 2. the other way around

___ 3. point of view

___ 4. multiply; amplify

___ 5. conversation

___ 6. compassionate

___ 7. of top importance

___ 8. component; aspect

___ 9. get used to; adjust

___ 10. disagreement; argument

B **Complete each sentence with a target word or phrase. Remember to use the correct word form.**

1. Traveling abroad can really help you _____.

2. As the store's prices kept rising, they _____ started losing customers.

3. A(n) _____ studies human cultures and the way they change over time.

4. The easiest way to _____ someone is by introducing yourself to him or her.

5. Movies sometimes spread _____ about a culture or race. They can affect the perspectives of people in other countries.

Part 1: Reading and Vocabulary Building

1   Friends are among the most important people in our lives. They provide companionship, a sense of belonging, and a **sympathetic** ear. As we work, study, and travel abroad, and even as we remain at home, we can also form friendships with people from other cultures. However, bridging cultural
5   differences is sometimes hard. Along with linguistic and historical issues, there are differences in body language, **conflict** management styles, and more.

Shared backgrounds and value systems make it easier to **befriend** people from our home countries. Yet, because these **elements** can't be taken for granted with people from other cultures, making friends with them can be challenging.
10 Learning to accept the differences that arise is easier said than done. According to **anthropologists** Kevin Avruch and Peter W. Black, people tend to view things they don't understand as wrong or strange. **Compounding** the problem are **stereotypes**, which are typically far from the truth. For instance, one stereotype about Americans is that they're all outgoing, whereas many are
15 actually quite **introverted**. So we should start by recognizing the stereotypes that we have, after which we can take steps to overcome them.

In doing so, having an open mind is **paramount**. If you say to a Parisian, "I know all French people are romantic," you might wind up insulting the person. It's better, then, to listen to your new friend talk about his or her life.
20 Naturally, he or she will also be curious about your background. Have respect for the differences that will **inevitably** arise. If you're interested in the sari worn by an Indian friend, tell her something about traditional clothing from your country. When in doubt, don't be afraid to ask questions. Over time, you'll become accustomed to your friend's style of dress, body language, and
25 speech patterns – and **vice-versa**.

Studying abroad (or making friends with international students in your home country) is an excellent way to **broaden your horizons**. Every year, millions

---

⁴ bridge – bring together; resolve differences
¹⁰ easier said than done – easy to talk about but difficult to do
²¹ sari – a type of long dress commonly worn by women in India

of people travel overseas for long or short courses of study. A local friend can guide you through the new culture while helping facilitate your social
30 adjustment. Studies have even found that integrating with the host culture can lead to lower stress levels and improved academic performance.

Many universities have programs which help international students **acclimatize**. For instance, at Tennessee State University,
35 in the USA, the Multicultural Friendship Society brings together American and international students. Once a month, they meet on campus for casual discussions. Once a year, the group puts on a Multicultural
40 Spring Celebration, an event attracting 300-400 people.

Differences in conflict management styles can complicate friendships.

Cross-cultural friendships are also important in countries which are home to multiple races. Though people from different cultural backgrounds may live in the same city, stereotyping and racism still occur. To help overcome such
45 issues, communities have youth programs which encourage **dialogue** while celebrating diversity. For example, in Australia, the Centre for Multicultural Youth runs programs that bring together young people from diverse backgrounds. In programs like these, young people learn to respect one another's points of view. Simply spending time together helps participants
50 see their new friends for the interesting and unique individuals that they are.

Efforts like these can have lasting benefits. Just getting to know one person from a different background broadens our world view. Indeed, though the world is becoming increasingly connected, that doesn't mean all cultures are blending into one. By forming a multicultural friendship, we form a
55 multicultural **perspective**. And that serves us well all through life, whether we're at work or school, online or offline, or at home or abroad.

---

30 integrate – become a part of
46 diversity – including people from many races and cultures

Choose the best answer.

.... **Main Idea**

1. (　) What is the main idea?
   A. Young people have an easy time forming cross-cultural friendships.
   B. Open-minded people enjoy getting to know others.
   C. Despite the challenges involved, multicultural friendships are worthwhile.
   D. Some schools bring local and foreign students together.

.... **Detail**

2. (　) What does the Multicultural Friendship Society do on an annual basis?
   A. They take a trip to Tennessee.　　B. They put on a play.
   C. They hold casual discussions.　　D. They arrange a festival.

.... **Vocabulary**

3. (　) In line 13, what does "far from the truth" mean?
   A. distant　　　　　B. inaccurate
   C. sincere　　　　　D. confusing

.... **Analysis**

4. (　) Why is it sometimes hard to form friendships across cultures?
   A. Our values may be very different.
   B. Everyone tries to keep an open mind.
   C. We know our stereotypes are valid.
   D. People from other cultures are unfriendly.

5. (　) What benefit of befriending locals while studying abroad is NOT discussed?
   A. Smoother social adjustment
   B. Better school grades
   C. Experiencing local holidays
   D. Lower stress levels

Short Answers **Answer each question based on the article.**

1. In Avruch and Black's judgment, how do we react to that which we don't understand?

   _____

2. According to the article, what should we do after recognizing our stereotypes?

   _____

3. What does the Centre for Multicultural Youth do?

   _____

Vocabulary Building

A **Choose the answer that means the same as the word in italics.**

1. The mining companies have started a *dialogue* on how they might work together to explore new finds.
   A. rivalry   B. discussion   C. investigation

2. I like talking to my grandmother about history since she has such an interesting *perspective*.
   A. lecture   B. outlook   C. souvenir

3. Securing the statue in place is *paramount*, since we don't want it to fall over.
   A. crucial   B. dangerous   C. engineered

4. It takes a few months to *acclimatize* to living in a new place.
   A. respond   B. attract   C. adjust

5. If we hire people when sales are down, won't it *compound* our problems?
   A. increase   B. simplify   C. redefine

B **Complete each sentence with the best word or phrase. Remember to use the correct word form.**

| befriend | vice-versa | element | anthropologist | broaden (one's) horizons |

1. It was very nice of you to _____ your new classmate.

2. In my opinion, trust is the most important _____ in a successful partnership.

3. If you want to _____, you can find a wealth of resources on the Internet.

4. Bob makes me laugh all the time, and _____. Other people think we're crazy.

5. When researching another culture, a(n) _____ might look into its history, customs, religions, and more.

C **Circle the correct form of each word.**

1. I can (sympathize/sympathy) with your wanting to live closer to work.

2. After a decade or two, a house will (inevitable/inevitably) start to show signs of wear.

3. The cartoon was criticized for containing (stereotype/stereotypical) images of Africans.

4. Matt is so (introverted/introvert) that he hasn't been to a party in years.

5. In some countries, fresh water rights are a source of (conflict/conflicting).

Part 2: Focus Areas

Focus on Language

Word Parts

Study the word parts in the chart. Then, read the following pairs of sentences. Circle if the second sentence is true or false.

Word Part	Meaning	Examples
intro/intra-	within	intravenous, intranet
-dem(o)-	people	demographics, endemic
-ous	full of	wondrous, malicious

1. Wild chimpanzees show a wide range of intraspecies variation.
   The animals are all so similar that it's hard to tell them apart. (True / False)

2. The H1N1 flu epidemic was headline news around the world.
   The epidemic received a considerable amount of attention. (True / False)

3. The container has the symbol for danger on it, so it may be hazardous.
   It may be unsafe to handle the contents without protective gear. (True / False)

Grammar   To do so & In doing so

These similar structures have completely different meanings. *To do so* is a phrase meaning "in order to accomplish something." *In doing so* is a phrase meaning "as something is done."

Ex: Scoring well on the GRE test is hard. To do so, people often study for months.

Ex: Doug sang at the top of his voice. In doing so, he woke up half the neighborhood.

Fill in each blank with *to do so* or *in doing so*.

1. We tried to fix the refrigerator light. However, _____, we accidentally broke one of the shelves.

2. Getting a hiking permit for the park is complex. _____, you need to fill out several forms.

3. I spent two years researching Swedish literature. _____, I also learned a lot about their history and culture.

4. He wants to become rich. _____, he'll have to work very hard.

Talk About It   **Discuss these questions in small groups.**

1. Even in the "Information Age" that we live in, stereotypes are common. Where do they come from? How can we overcome them?

2. If you don't have a chance to travel or study abroad, how else can you make friends with people from other countries?

3. People studying overseas often have trouble adjusting. If you were the director of a school, how would you make their adjustment easier?

Write About It

Question: Over time, will the world's cultures become more similar, or will they retain their uniqueness? Give two reasons to support your opinion. Prepare by writing notes on the lines below. The first few words of the paragraph are written to help you get started.

Opinion: _____

Reason 1: _____

Reason 2: _____

In the future, the world's cultures will _____

_____

_____

_____

_____

_____

_____

_____

Focus on Testing

Listening Listen to the announcement. Then, answer the following questions.

Track 39

1. (　) What is this announcement probably advertising?
   (A) A radio program
   (B) A public protest
   (C) A university course
   (D) A crisis hotline

2. (　) What will take place last?
   (A) Two students will tell their stories.
   (B) Some listeners will ask questions.
   (C) A researcher will give his perspective.
   (D) Conflict resolution will be discussed.

3. (　) Where is Hans Schmidt originally from?
   (A) Brazil   (B) Canada
   (C) Germany   (D) Greece

Reading Choose the correct word(s) to fill in each blank.

As a growing percentage of our friendships are formed online, social scientists are curious whether that's changing the nature of friendship. One study at Albright College examined an ingredient (___1___) paramount to friendship building: trust. Researchers supplied 10 volunteers with microphones and asked them to record face to face dialogues with friends. Participants also kept records of their online chats, instant messages, and forum posts. After two weeks, the spoken and written material was collected and analyzed. The researchers discovered (___2___) on the Net, people shared more personal details about themselves, whereas in face to face meetings, people made more personal comments about their friends. Both elements are critical in building trust, yet they revealed (___3___) to different degrees offline and online.

1. (　) (A) consider   (B) to consider
        (C) considering   (D) considered

2. (　) (A) which   (B) whom
        (C) where   (D) that

3. (　) (A) themselves   (B) them
        (C) their   (D) theirs

100

Supplementary Reading - *The Peace Corps*

 Track 40

Many opportunities exist for people who want to travel abroad to experience a foreign culture. Homestays, study abroad programs, student exchanges, and international competitions all offer rich opportunities for cross-cultural interaction. There are also government-run programs, such as the Peace Corps. Established by US president John F. Kennedy in 1961, the organization has sent volunteers all over the globe to take part in community enriching programs.

Since its inception four decades ago, the Peace Corps has sent 200,000 Americans abroad. They've traveled to 139 countries, with the majority serving in Africa and Latin America. Volunteers commit to 27 months of service, which includes pre-service training and time spent overseas. Their assignments may be in one of many fields, such as education, agriculture, health, business, and youth development. Since many of these fields require specialized knowledge, 89% of volunteers hold university degrees.

The hard work of Peace Corps volunteers has a real impact on the places they serve. On a community level, the wells they dig supply fresh water to entire villages. On a personal level, the individuals they teach can go on to do great things. For instance, in the Dominican Republic, a young boy who was taught English by Peace Corps volunteers later became the president of his country. Likewise, Americans who have given their time have aspired to greatness, pursuing careers in education, the arts, and government service. One US congressman who volunteered in Senegal called being in the Peace Corps one of the most important experiences of his life.

Read each sentence. Circle if it is true (T) or false (F).

1. The Peace Corps was set up by a private organization. T / F
2. Volunteers must devote more than two years of their time. T / F
3. Less than one-half of all participants are college educated. T / F
4. Beneficiaries of Peace Corps programs have gone on to become national leaders. T / F
5. Some Peace Corps volunteers have done extraordinary things with their lives. T / F

11 Health

Muscle Memory

Many of our daily actions involve habits and skills which take a long time to master. Muscle memory plays a key role in developing those skills. It's also an important factor in understanding many psychological problems. Once we understand the process of muscle memory, we can use it to our advantage.

Pre-Reading Questions Discuss these questions in pairs.

1. What are you skilled at doing?

2. Have you ever played any sports? How much practice time was required?

3. Have you ever had the experience of getting nervous, happy, or sad just by remembering something? Can you think of any examples?

Vocabulary Warmup ◉ Track 41

A **Listen to the unit's target vocabulary. Then, write the letter of the correct word or phrase next to each definition.**

a. accomplish	f. interrupt	k. rhythm
b. appropriate	g. precision	l. slump
c. conscious	h. proficient	m. tense up
d. crawl	i. pulse	n. trigger
e. criticism	j. resolve	o. utmost

___ 1. skilled; able

___ 2. negative or contrary opinion

___ 3. aware; awake

___ 4. achieve

___ 5. accuracy

___ 6. to the greatest degree; extreme

___ 7. move around on one's hands and legs

___ 8. settle; fix

___ 9. suitable

___ 10. initiate; cause

B **Complete each sentence with a target word or phrase. Remember to use the correct word form.**

1. The baseball player's _____ was so severe that he saw a sports psychologist to help him get over it.

2. At the scene of an accident, one of the first things an emergency responder does is take the victim's _____.

3. As it floated down the river, the boat rocked back and forth with a gentle _____.

4. When standing in front of a large audience, even experienced speakers can _____ and forget what they planned to say.

5. Television shows are sometimes _____ by important news broadcasts.

Part 1: Reading and Vocabulary Building

Reading Passage Track 42

1   Much of what we do is habitual. When we brush our teeth, walk down
the street, and interact with friends, we are, to a large degree, repeating
learned actions and behaviors. At the core of this is muscle memory, which
describes the mind-body interaction that leads to habit formation and skill
5   development. The phenomenon applies to our physical, emotional, and
social lives. Thus, understanding the process can go a long way towards
resolving personal and interpersonal issues.

What exactly is muscle memory? Every time we perform an action, our
brain sends commands to the **appropriate** muscles via the central nervous
10 system. The first time we do something – say go bowling – our muscles
aren't accustomed to the action, and we tend to perform poorly. However,
as the action is repeated, the neural pathway from the brain to the muscles
is strengthened, improving our skill level. The establishment of a specific
neural pattern can be defined as muscle memory. Over time, the movement
15 requires less **conscious** thought, and we become so **proficient** that the action
can be performed subconsciously. This is the concept of "automaticity."

The process literally begins from our earliest days. After we're born, we're
nearly helpless. Newborns are unable to walk, **crawl**, talk, or protect
themselves. It takes years to master all the necessary skills for daily life.
20 Even simple actions which we take for granted, such as using a spoon and
brushing our teeth, require choreographed ballets of motor skills which must
be practiced repeatedly before they're perfected.

For those who perform specialized skills, developing automaticity is of the
utmost importance. Top athletes like LeBron James and Alex Rodriguez
25 spend countless hours practicing the same movements. When it's time to
compete, actions such as shooting a basketball and swinging a bat can be
performed with a high degree of **precision**. Indeed, when athletes find
themselves in a "**slump**," it can be caused by "over thinking." That is, by

---

² to a large degree – for the most part
⁵ phenomenon – movement; trend; happening
¹² neural – related to the nervous system
¹⁶ subconsciously – done without a person's awareness
²¹ choreographed – involving a precise sequence of movements

consciously questioning themselves, they **interrupt** the subconscious mind-
30   muscle **rhythm**.

For people with psychological problems,
it's easy to think oneself into trouble. That's
because along with memories of what we've
seen and done, the part of the brain called the
35   amygdala stores the physiological responses
to past emotional experiences. So, for people
who stutter, for instance, facial muscles **tense
up** just before they speak. When it comes time
to talk to someone, the experience can cause
40   nervousness, an emotional state **triggering** the same physiological response.

For successful athletes, muscle memory is of key importance.

The situation can be even more serious for people who experience panic
attacks. Just thinking or worrying about something can trigger a faster
pulse, higher blood pressure, and chest pains. Likewise, people suffering
from post traumatic stress disorder may face a daily struggle to get through
45   life. For them, the traumatic event was so powerful that it established a long-
lasting mind-muscle pathway. Even non-threatening situations, because
they remind the person of the traumatic experience, can trigger a strong
physiological response.

One can even see muscle memory at work in our social interactions. Our
50   responses to common questions, the way we deal with **criticism**, and
many other actions are the result of mentally conditioned habits. Even
an organization can be said to operate with its own muscle memory, if
it regularly responds to challenges in a habitual fashion. The key to self-
improvement is to identify problematic habits and slowly correct them.
55   That can be **accomplished** by forming new responses to old situations – in
other words, by creating new neural pathways leading to more favorable
responses. Indeed, once we understand how muscle memory works, it can
be put to very good use.

---

35 physiological – related to the body
37 stutter – repeat a sound over and over, while having trouble speaking naturally
51 conditioned – formed out of habit or training

Choose the best answer.

.... Main Idea

1. (   ) What is the main idea?
   A. Muscle memory can help explain our actions and emotional states.
   B. Newborns have very active muscle memory networks.
   C. To understand muscle memory, we should focus on the amygdala.
   D. Post traumatic stress disorder and muscle memory are linked.

.... Detail

2. (   ) What strengthens neural pathways to muscles?
   A. Constantly thinking about something
   B. Performing an action over and over
   C. Restating a command many times
   D. Frequently watching an expert practice

.... Vocabulary

3. (   ) In line 11, what does "accustomed to" mean?
   A. familiar with   B. related to
   C. aware of   D. introduced by

.... Analysis

4. (   ) What is implied about common actions like getting dressed?
   A. Since they're so easy, they require almost no time to learn.
   B. We're helpless if we're unable to carry out such actions.
   C. People who study ballet perform them more gracefully.
   D. They put to use well-developed muscle memory patterns.

5. (   ) According to the article, what can cause an athlete's slump?
   A. Spending too much time practicing the same movements.
   B. Letting conscious thoughts interfere with a skill's automaticity.
   C. Developing such precision that one's performance is flawless.
   D. Forgetting to store physiological responses in the amygdala.

Short Answers   Answer each question based on the article.

1. How does the brain send commands to the muscles?

   _____

2. What happens when someone has a panic attack?

   _____

3. According to the article, how can we correct bad habits?

   _____

Vocabulary Building

A **Choose the answer that means the same as the word in italics.**

1. Mr. Billiton, a very *proficient* analyst, will be assisting you with the case.
   A. respected   B. in-demand   C. capable

2. Movie-goers had a hard time remaining *conscious* during the five-hour epic.
   A. interested   B. awake   C. hungry

3. The musical composition has a *rhythm* that's sometimes fast and sometimes slow.
   A. flow   B. scope   C. goal

4. With so many applicants, you'll need to put your *utmost* effort into getting the job.
   A. financial   B. common   C. maximum

5. Do you think the novel is *appropriate* for 9th grade students?
   A. fitting   B. surprising   C. interesting

B **Complete each sentence with the best word or phrase. Remember to use the correct word form.**

tense up	crawl	trigger	pulse	slump

1. One way to take a person's _____ is by touching his or her neck.

2. Before a baby walks, it learns to sit up and _____.

3. Officials are worried an earthquake could _____ a landslide.

4. Even the best salespeople go through _____ during which they have trouble making a sale.

5. It's easy to _____ before an important test.

C **Circle the correct form of each word.**

1. I apologize for the (interruption/interrupt). I get a lot of phone calls at this time of day.

2. The club passed a (resolve/resolution) requiring members to attend every meeting.

3. The mayor called the gold medal winner to congratulate her on her (accomplish/accomplishment).

4. If you're going to be (critical/criticism) of the rule, you should be prepared to say why.

5. Rolex watches are famous for their (precise/precision) and craftsmanship.

Part 2: Focus Areas

Focus on Language

Word Parts

Study the word parts in the chart. Then, read the following pairs of sentences. Circle if the second sentence is true or false.

Word Part	Meaning	Examples
sub-	beneath	submarine, substandard
-cis-	cut	decisive, excise
-ence	state; action	deference, confidence

1. Alice Reed doesn't allow subordinates to address her by her first name.
   Members of Ms. Reed's staff can call her "Alice." (True / False)

2. The machine is so precise that it cuts metal with a 99.99% level of accuracy.
   Nearly flawless results can be achieved using the metal cutter. (True / False)

3. Vera showed persistence in setting up an interview with the president.
   Arranging the interview took a lot of effort. (True / False)

Grammar *Reflexive Pronouns*

We often use reflexive pronouns (myself, herself, etc.) to say something about the subject of a sentence or clause. They're useful when telling stories and describing actions.

Structure: I – myself   he – himself   she – herself
            we – ourselves   they – themselves   it – itself
            you – yourself (singular) / yourselves (plural)

Ex: I think we can probably finish painting the fence by ourselves.

Ex: During the boring speech, Christine found herself falling asleep.

Fill in each blank with a reflexive pronoun.

1. I need a hand with this box. I can't lift it by _____.

2. If I can't make it to the party, I hope you guys enjoy _____.

3. Boris and Ileana told _____ they'd only stay in New York a few months, but they wound up living there for three years.

4. Since our friends don't have time to help us move, we'll have to take care of everything _____.

Talk About It   **Discuss these questions in small groups.**

1. Have you ever learned a skill (such as a sport or instrument) so well that you were able to perform it with a high degree of automaticity? What is it?

2. Do you have any bad habits? Talk about one of them.

3. Deep down, do you think it's possible for people to change their personalities? If so, how?

Write About It

Question: Do you think that, with practice, it's possible for a person to learn any skill? Give two reasons to support your opinion. Prepare by writing notes on the lines below. The first few words of the paragraph are written to help you get started.

Opinion: _____

Reason 1: _____

Reason 2: _____

When it comes to learning a new skill, I think _____

_____

_____

_____

_____

_____

_____

_____

Listening Listen to the conversation. Then, answer the following questions.

Track 43

1. (   ) Where is Greg?
   (A) At an accident scene   (B) At the office
   (C) At his house   (D) At a bike shop

2. (   ) What was the woman's first reaction to the accident?
   (A) She quickly ran over.   (B) She didn't move.
   (C) She made a phone call.   (D) She fell down.

3. (   ) What will the woman probably do next?
   (A) Drive to the hospital   (B) Contact emergency services
   (C) Have a meal with Greg   (D) Call a restaurant

Reading Read the passage. Then, answer the following questions.

Between work, family, and friends, you're busier than ever, and while getting in shape sounds like a great idea, you just haven't got the time. At Easy Gym, we understand that. Designed for people with full schedules, Easy Gym can help you build up those abs and flatten that stomach with a minimal time commitment. Our fitness experts have created 10 programs to choose from, each of which involves two weekly workouts lasting just 20 minutes each. With our precision exercise equipment and carefully designed aerobic programs, you'll become a better you in no time at all. Our seven locations in San Francisco make it easy to find a nearby location. So if you have the resolve to get in shape, we can help you accomplish your goal, starting today!

1. (   ) What is the purpose of the passage?
   (A) To provide a warning   (B) To discourage a habit
   (C) To advertise a service   (D) To issue a report

2. (   ) What is suggested about the target readers?
   (A) They have little time for physical fitness.
   (B) They mostly want to improve their abs.
   (C) They all work in the same part of the city.
   (D) They don't need to use precision equipment.

3. (   ) What piece of information is NOT included?
   (A) The name of the company   (B) The price of the programs
   (C) The number of locations   (D) The frequency of the workouts

Supplementary Reading - *Weightlifting*

 Track 44

Weight resistance training has looked more closely at the issue of muscle memory than many other sports. That's perhaps not surprising, since its objective is to increase muscle mass while improving one's form. The first time a person trains, considerable effort is put into building muscle mass (known as "hypertrophy"). When a person takes a break – or "detrains" – for a period of time, the muscles shrink (or "atrophy"). However, once the person starts training again, it takes him or her less time to regain previous levels of muscle mass. It appears as if the muscles have retained a "memory" of their previous state. What exactly is happening?

On a basic level, the first time a person trains, he or she isn't accustomed to the workout routine. During the learning process, one's body requires time and effort to learn the lifting movements and  become accustomed to ever-increasing weight loads. Returning to a routine after a period of inactivity requires less effort, since a person's body is already primed to achieve a certain fitness level.

Also, as someone trains, neural connections to the target muscles are strengthened. Plus, more muscle fibers are used as weight loads increase. Even after detraining for several months, a weightlifter retains the potential to recapture those gains. Research into muscle fibers and proteins has revealed that weightlifters, after detraining, retain a high percentage of certain proteins which are key to muscle fiber growth. Thus, when weightlifters start training again, hypertrophy is more easily achieved.

Read each sentence. Circle if it is true (T) or false (F).

1. Hypertrophy is the process of losing muscle mass after you stop working out. T / F
2. After a period of detraining, weightlifters who start training again have an easier time rebuilding muscle mass. T / F
3. Learning weightlifting movements does not contribute to the difficulty of establishing a workout routine. T / F
4. The relationship between weight loads and fiber growth is unclear. T / F
5. Certain proteins are advantageous in regrowing muscle fibers. T / F

12

Maritime Piracy

Modern pirates, equipped with guns and speed boats, continue attacking vessels in the world's busiest shipping lanes. Because merchant ships can rarely defend themselves, they make easy targets. Governments, backed by the UN, are taking measures against the growing threat.

Pre-Reading Questions Discuss these questions in pairs.

1. Have you heard of any cases of modern piracy? If so, where did they take place?

2. Why do pirates attack ships?

3. How can ships protect themselves against pirates?

Vocabulary Warmup Track 45

A Listen to the unit's target vocabulary. Then, write the letter of the correct word or phrase next to each definition.

a. catastrophe	f. lethal	k. provoke
b. collide	g. merchant	l. ransom
c. dispatch	h. motive	m. the lion's share
d. hijack	i. port	n. vulnerable
e. incident	j. prone to	o. ward off

___ 1. likely to; inclined to

___ 2. seller; trader

___ 3. event; occasion

___ 4. bump or crash into

___ 5. harbor

___ 6. largest percentage; great majority

___ 7. reason; purpose

___ 8. deadly

___ 9. at risk; weak

___ 10. disaster

B Complete each sentence with a target word or phrase. Remember to use the correct word form.

1. It's unwise to _____ a stray dog, no matter how small it is.

2. After sales at the Remington branch fell for a third year, the company _____ its top manager to deal with the situation.

3. The criminals demanded a $5 million _____ for the release of the hostages.

4. Safety measures on airplanes make it difficult to _____ a plane, but it still does happen from time to time.

5. A good way to _____ colds is by washing your hands often.

Part 1: Reading and Vocabulary Building

1 The word "pirate" often conjures up images of sailors with eye patches and parrots on their shoulders. The truth is, modern piracy is anything but heroic. It's a deadly business that threatens thousands of lives and costs companies billions of dollars. Unfortunately, the search for solutions
5 has proven difficult. In the 21ˢᵗ century, we still rely on the oceans for transportation, with some 80% of the world's goods shipped by sea. Valuable ships and their cargo make attractive targets for pirates, whose numbers are growing.

Maritime piracy dates back many centuries, with **incidents** recorded as far
10 back as 3,000 years ago. In ancient times, pirates hid along rocky coasts and attacked passing **merchant** ships. Several areas in the Mediterranean Sea, including Cilicia (in modern Turkey), were centers of pirate activity. These days, pirates have faster ships and better weapons, but their primary **motive** remains the same: profit. Usually, between 5-10 people are involved in an
15 attack, which may aim to seize cargo, kidnap crew members for **ransom**, or **hijack** the ship. Attacks may take place in a **port**, in territorial waters near a nation's coast, or in international waters.

As in ancient times, modern pirates track vessels in the world's major shipping lanes. Areas **prone to** attack include the Malacca Strait (between
20 Indonesia and Malaysia), the Gulf of Guinea (near Nigeria), and the Gulf of Aden (near Somalia). Such places are especially **vulnerable** since the narrow lanes force ships to proceed at a slower pace.

The number of incidents is on the rise. Between 1994 and 1999, there were an average of 209 attacks per year. That rose to an average of 352 between 2000
25 and 2008. The Horn of Africa and Gulf of Aden have seen **the lion's share** of recent incidents. In 2008, a full 37% of the world's pirate attacks took place in the region. Several cases that year were spectacular, including the hijacking

---

¹ conjure up – cause to appear; make someone think of something
⁹ maritime – related to the ocean
⁹ as far back as – dating back to
¹⁵ kidnap – hold a person against his or her will
¹⁶ territorial – belonging to a place, country, etc.
²⁷ spectacular – incredible

of a ship carrying Russian tanks. The same year, Somali pirates seized a Saudi Arabian supertanker, later handing it back for an estimated $3 million.

30 Unfortunately, ships have a limited ability to **ward off** attacks. Modern vessels often carry small crews of less than 10 people. What's more, the Maritime Safety Commission discourages ships from arming themselves since it may **provoke** pirates into using deadly force. In the face of an attack, vessels are encouraged to try to outrun pursuers. Electrical fences can also

35 be installed around a ship to make boarding difficult. Plus, ships can carry non-**lethal** weapons such as high-pressure water hoses and ear-piercing loudspeakers.

Multinational efforts to combat piracy are also effective deterrents. In 2008, the United

40 Nations passed four resolutions allowing ships to pursue pirates into Somalian waters and onto land. Furthermore, a number of warships, including vessels from NATO, the EU, and countries including China and the USA, have

45 been **dispatched** to patrol the troubled area.

The use of military force is one way nations have responded to piracy.

Regional agreements can also have an impact. In 2004, 16 Asian countries signed the Regional Cooperation Agreement on Combating Piracy and Armed Robbery against Ships in Asia (ReCAPP). The pact, which involves information sharing and coordinated anti-piracy efforts, is credited with

50 helping reduce the problem in Southeast Asia.

In the fight against piracy, the stakes are high, as maritime trade is worth trillions of dollars. Piracy disrupts the worldwide flow of goods while endangering the lives of crewmembers. Attacks also pose an environmental risk, and observers fear a **catastrophe** may occur should an oil tanker **collide**

55 with a pirate ship. Modern maritime piracy may not be heroic, nor may it feature in Hollywood movies, but it remains a key global security issue.

---

29 supertanker – very large ship used to transport oil
36 ear-piercing – causing extreme pain to someone's ears
39 deterrent – something that discourages an action or behavior
40 resolution – strong decision or conclusion
48 pact – agreement
51 stakes – that which is at risk

.... **Main Idea**

1. (   ) What is the main idea?

    A. Piracy in the world's oceans is still a threat to international trade.

    B. In ancient times, piracy was more heroic than it now is.

    C. We rely on sea transport to ship cargo around the world.

    D. Maritime piracy is common in the waters off the Somalian coast.

.... **Detail**

2. (   ) Above all, what motivates pirates to seize ships?

    A. Status   B. Property

    C. Money   D. Revenge

.... **Vocabulary**

3. (   ) In line 41, what does "pursue" mean?

    A. attack   B. chase

    C. threaten   D. deter

.... **Analysis**

4. (   ) Why are commercial ship captains advised against carrying weapons?

    A. It could lead to violent behavior from pirates.

    B. Pirates always carry larger and deadlier weapons.

    C. It's illegal to carry guns on commercial vessels.

    D. Weapons cost more than electrical fences.

5. (   ) What does the article imply about regional agreements against piracy?

    A. They can be effective counter-measures.

    B. They are being coordinated by the United Nations.

    C. They will soon be tested in Southeast Asia.

    D. They rely on the participation of NATO warships.

Short Answers   Answer each question based on the article.

1. Globally, what percentage of goods is transported on the world's oceans?

_____

2. How are modern pirates different from ancient pirates?

_____

3. Why do major shipping lanes experience so many pirate attacks?

_____

Vocabulary Building

A Choose the answer that means the same as the word or phrase in italics.

1. *Merchants* along the pier are delighted that the city will host a boat race.
   A. Ship builders   B. Shop owners   C. Sports fans

2. By shouting and waving their hands, they were able to *ward off* the tiger.
   A. chase away   B. calm down   C. care for

3. Retail stores treat *incidents* of theft as a cost of doing business.
   A. frequencies   B. occurrences   C. consequences

4. If the wall is *vulnerable* to floods, you should have it reinforced before the next storm.
   A. at risk   B. in lieu   C. on track

5. *The lion's share* of people in New York City take the subway to work.
   A. The residents   B. The majority   C. The preference

B Complete each sentence with the best word or phrase. Remember to use the correct word form.

lethal	prone to	ransom	hijack	port

1. A _____ note was found in the kidnap victim's hotel room.

2. Boats using the _____ pay a one-time registration fee and a yearly service fee.

3. Few snake bites are _____, but many are quite painful.

4. Since the area is _____ heavy rains, most residents carry an umbrella at all times.

5. Whereas pirates once used knives to _____ vessels, many now carry guns.

C Circle the correct form of each word.

1. Airplanes carry sophisticated instruments to avoid (collide/colliding) with other aircraft.

2. Kyle is smart, but does he have the (motivate/motivation) to run a business?

3. I don't think someone bumping into you is sufficient (provocation/provoke) to start a fight.

4. If Lester joins one of our rivals, it will be (catastrophe/catastrophic).

5. (Dispatch/Dispatching) two detectives to the site to look for any evidence of wrongdoing.

Part 2: Focus Areas

Focus on Language

Word Parts

Study the word parts in the chart. Then, read the following pairs of sentences. Circle if the second sentence is true or false.

Word Part	Meaning	Examples
out-	exceed; beyond	outperform, outclass
-mar-	sea	mariner, aquamarine
-age	action	marriage, passage

1. With his superior speed, the runner outdistanced himself from the pack.
   The athlete ran well ahead of his competitors. (True / False)

2. The California coast is well known for its rich marine life.
   The area is famous for its land animals. (True / False)

3. Sarah is uncertain she'll have the courage to deliver the speech.
   She's confident the speech will turn out well. (True / False)

Grammar   *Conditional sentences with "should"*

Conditional sentences are used to state a possible outcome, given a set of conditions. *Should* is often used in formal English for emphasis. It can appear before or after the clause's subject.
Structure: **If s + should + v, s + v** *or* **Should + s + v, s + (will/would) + v**
Ex: If you should run into trouble, please let me know.
Ex: Should the factory close, a lot of people will lose their jobs.

Combine the two sentences using *should*.

1. You might need help. In that case, feel free to call me.

   _____

2. The drought may continue. In that case, many crops will die.

   _____

3. An accident may occur. In that case, the results would be deadly.

   _____

118

Talk About It   **Discuss these questions in small groups.**

1. What's the best way to reduce the number of pirate attacks?

2. Should crew members receive more pay if their route takes them through dangerous waters (like the Gulf of Aden)? Why or why not?

3. What would you do if your ship were attacked by pirates? Would you give them the ship or fight back?

Write About It

Question: Should ships' crews carry weapons (like guns) to defend themselves? Give two reasons to support your opinion. Prepare by writing notes on the lines below. The first few words of the paragraph are written to help you get started.

Opinion: _____

Reason 1: _____

Reason 2: _____

Carrying weapons for defensive purposes _____

_____

_____

_____

_____

_____

_____

_____

_____

Focus on Testing

Listening Listen to the speech. Then, answer the following questions.

Track 47

1. (   ) What is this speech announcing?
   (A) A promotion
   (B) An accident
   (C) A retirement
   (D) An assignment

2. (   ) What does the speaker suggest about the company?
   (A) It is owned by Leonard Mitchell.
   (B) It delivers cargo via truck.
   (C) It was founded several years ago.
   (D) It started off very small.

3. (   ) How does the speaker describe Captain Mitchell?
   (A) Reliable   (B) Fierce
   (C) Humble   (D) Funny

Reading Choose the correct word(s) to fill in each blank.

Because of their valuable cargos and minimal defenses, merchant ships make especially attractive targets for maritime pirates. In response, some private companies offer security services to bolster ships' (___1___) capabilities. Vessels can hire armed security personnel to accompany them on voyages. Or, an escort vessel can be hired to traverse dangerous shipping lanes. Because of the high risk and expense (___2___) the latter service, it's an option which would likely only be used by ships carrying rare or valuable cargo. In fact, many shipping firms choose to forego any additional security measures, opting instead to simply pay the ransom should one of their vessels (___3___) hijacked. Unfortunately, critics say, doing so emboldens hijackers and encourages piracy.

1. (   ) (A) defensively   (B) defend
         (C) defensiveness   (D) defensive

2. (   ) (A) associated with (B) extracted from
         (C) manipulated by   (D) reliant on

3. (   ) (A) being   (B) be
         (C) to be   (D) was

120

Supplementary Reading - *The Case of Somalia* Track 48

Somalia has become nearly synonymous with maritime piracy. Over the last decade, the Gulf of Aden has seen hundreds of pirate attacks. Events like the hijacking of supertankers, chemical tankers, and other ships have made global headlines. In fact, in just a single week in January 2010, four vessels from Greece, England, and Singapore were hijacked.

Why is Somalia such a hub of piracy? Two critical factors are the widespread poverty and lack of a stable government. Somalia has been ravaged by war for years, and gangs with enough firepower can enter and leave ports at will. Ransoms can net pirates millions of dollars, so they view the potential payoff as worth the risk.

Complicating the situation is the fact that millions of Somalis rely on food donations from foreign relief organizations. Ninety percent of that aid enters the country via water, making the Gulf of Aden's security a matter of life and death. Cargo ships can't avoid the Gulf either, as it leads to the Suez Canal. An astounding 22,000 ships go through the canal every year, representing 12% of the world's sea trade.

In response to the crisis, the UN has passed several security resolutions, and more than a dozen countries have sent warships to the area. The UN has also put together a set of "best management practice" guidelines for commercial ships. They include adding barbed wire around vessels, placing boards at ship entry points, and other defensive measures. According to officials, ships which adopt the guidelines are far less likely to be attacked by pirates.

Read each sentence. Circle if it is true (T) or false (F).

1. World governments and the UN feel Somalia should solve its   T / F
   piracy problems by itself.

2. Ransom payoffs give pirates the incentive to hijack more ships.   T / F

3. Most charitable donations to Somalia are shipped overland.   T / F

4. Cargo vessels can easily bypass the Gulf of Aden.   T / F

5. Following the UN's "best management practice" guidelines can   T / F
   help protect ships.

13 Identity

The Science of Love

Love is the subject of countless songs, poems, and stories. Researchers are now using scientific methods to uncover some of the secrets of attraction. Brain scans and other advanced techniques are helping them determine how the brain reacts to being in love.

Pre-Reading Questions ▸ Discuss these questions in pairs.

1. What attracts one person to another? (appearance? job? something else?)

2. How do people behave when they're in love?

3. Are new relationships different from long-term relationships? If so, how?

Vocabulary Warmup Track 49

A Listen to the unit's target vocabulary. Then, write the letter of the correct word or phrase next to each definition.

a. activate	f. fixate	k. palm
b. elated	g. hormone	l. passion
c. elevated	h. indicate	m. potion
d. fascinating	i. instantly	n. prominence
e. figure of speech	j. nurturing	o. substance

___ 1. importance

___ 2. demonstrate; show

___ 3. material

___ 4. very happy

___ 5. focus on

___ 6. very interesting

___ 7. turn on; trigger

___ 8. raised; higher

___ 9. immediately

___ 10. saying; expression

B Complete each sentence with a target word or phrase. Remember to use the correct word form.

1. Some people think the lines on your _____ hold the secrets to your future.

2. Since the athlete plays with energy and _____, he has a lot of fans.

3. In the movie, the witch gives the princess a(n) _____ that makes her fall asleep.

4. If a person's _____ are imbalanced, he or she may have emotional problems.

5. Babies with _____ mothers tend to grow up to be caring people themselves.

Part 1: Reading and Vocabulary Building

1   It has been said that "love makes the world go round." That may be truer
than we realize. Scientific interest in romantic love has turned up **fascinating**
discoveries about the physiology of love, including the mapping out of
several processes of physical attraction. The sweaty palms and quickened
5   heartbeats of lovers have been linked to the production of specific hormones
and neurotransmitters. Thus, when we talk about two people "having
chemistry," it's not just a **figure of speech**.

Another popular saying is "beauty is in the eye of the beholder." Concepts
of beauty certainly vary among cultures and individuals, but what fascinates
10 scientists are the mental activities behind the eyes. One study at the
University of Rochester focused on clothing color. Men were shown a photo
of a woman wearing a red dress, as well as a photo of the same woman in a
blue dress. Participants were asked how much they'd spend on a date, with
results linking a higher amount to the red dress photo. The findings correlate
15 with other studies, as well as the **prominence** of the color on holidays like
Valentine's Day.

Another study at Florida State University showed just how much power
attractive people hold over us. Participants were shown photos of beautiful
women and handsome men, after which they were told to look away from
20 the images. The study's first finding was that we are **instantly** drawn to
attractive people – in fact, it took less than half a second for participants to
fixate on each photo. Researchers also found that people had trouble pulling
their eyes away from the images, **indicating** the degree to which "animal
magnetism" is at work.

25 When everything comes together and we fall in love, our **palms** get sweaty,
we have trouble sleeping, and we can't stop thinking about that special
someone. What's going on here? In its early stages, romantic love leads to

---

⁶ neurotransmitter – a type of brain chemical
⁶ have chemistry – people who "have chemistry" are well matched for each other
⁸ beholder – person who sees something
¹⁴ correlate with – line up with; correspond to
²³ animal magnetism – the physical attraction that draws two people together

a higher production of certain brain chemicals, including dopamine and
phenylethylamine, as well as hormones like adrenaline and norepinephrine.
30 This powerful mixture gives us more energy, focuses our attention, and
makes us feel **elated**. Our bodies are primed for courtship.

A detailed study of 2,500 brain scans revealed even more. Seventeen people
were shown photos of people they were in love with. Just looking at the
images **activated** specific brain regions (such as the ventral tegmental area)
35 which are associated with addiction and pleasure. Such areas are also high
in neurotransmitters like dopamine. It's no wonder being in love is often
compared to mental instability. In some ways, the effects are the same!

Within 1-3 years, as people settle into a more stable relationship, these
chemicals return to normal levels. Yet that isn't the end of love's impact.
40 People in long-term relationships show
elevated levels of oxytocin, a **hormone**
associated with forming **nurturing** bonds
and maintaining trust. Another brain
chemical, serotonin (which is associated with
45 calmness), is also higher during this period.
MRI scans have revealed that even after 20
years of marriage, people show increased
activity in regions associated with these
substances.

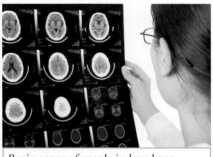

*Brain scans of people in love have
yielded interesting findings.*

50 Given all these discoveries, some scientists feel it will one day be possible to
create love **potions** which will make it easier to fall in love or rekindle the
passion in a marriage. So far, though, no "magic formula" has been found,
despite the efforts of perfume companies worldwide. Scientists are also
quick to point out that love is a complex process, with many factors involved
55 in finding and keeping a partner. So, for all the romantics out there, take
heart – love poems, boxes of chocolate, and long walks on the beach will still
be capturing hearts for years to come.

---

[31] courtship – dating; trying to win someone's affection
[51] rekindle – relight; raise interest once again
[55] take heart – feel confident; don't worry

.... **Main Idea**

   1. (   ) What is the main idea?
      A. Every culture has different ideas about love.
      B. Sweaty palms are caused by the release of neurotransmitters.
      C. We know so much about love that romance has lost its meaning.
      D. Scientific research has taught us a lot about love.

.... **Detail**

   2. (   ) Which substance is linked to long-term romance?
      A. Dopamine   B. Serotonin
      C. Adrenaline   D. Norepinephrine

.... **Vocabulary**

   3. (   ) In line 31, what does "primed" mean?
      A. assigned   B. achieved
      C. prepared   D. shocked

.... **Analysis**

   4. (   ) According to the article, how are love and mental instability alike?
      A. Both mental states lead to irregular heartbeats.
      B. They can both be linked to increased activity in parts of the brain.
      C. The conditions are both associated with high serotonin levels.
      D. Love always leads to madness, and vice-versa.

   5. (   ) What does the article suggest about the development of a "love potion"?
      A. Perfume companies feel the effort is a waste of money.
      B. It's easier to create than a magic formula.
      C. Scientists have not yet accomplished the task.
      D. Such a potion would only be effective on single people.

Short Answers **Answer each question based on the article.**

1. In the Florida State study, how long did it take people to fixate on a photo?

   _____

2. What effects do dopamine and other "romantic love chemicals" have on us?

   _____

3. What is the role of oxytocin in our bodies?

   _____

Vocabulary Building

A Choose the answer that means the same as the word or phrase in italics.

1. It was just a *figure of speech* and wasn't meant to be taken literally.
   A. emotion   B. opinion   C. saying

2. It's hard to *fixate* on a goal if you're doing 10 different things at once.
   A. activate   B. appreciate   C. concentrate

3. Investigators are uncertain what the mysterious *substance* is.
   A. material   B. stranger   C. remedy

4. Allen has had a *passion* for science since his parents gave him a chemistry set on his tenth birthday.
   A. research   B. enthusiasm   C. ability

5. Drinking a lot of coffee can lead to an *elevated* heart rate.
   A. increased   B. suspicious   C. legitimate

B Complete each sentence with the best word. Remember to use the correct word form.

hormone	fascinating	palm	nurturing	potion

1. When I'm in the middle of a _____ book, I have trouble putting it down.

2. The magician says drinking the _____ will make you invisible!

3. People with _____ personalities make very good parents.

4. Some _____, like oxytocin, are associated with positive emotional states.

5. Put the seeds in the _____ of your hand, and the deer will let you feed it.

C Circle the correct form of each word.

1. Martin was absolutely (elated/elation) to win the election.

2. This (indicate/indicator) light will tell you if the engine is too hot.

3. (Activate/Activating) the cell phone's pre-paid card only takes a minute.

4. The problem with hiring (prominence/prominent) lawyers is their fees tend to be high.

5. The Internet has made people accustomed to getting what they want (instantly/instant).

Part 2: Focus Areas

Focus on Language

Word Parts

Study the word parts in the chart. Then, read the following pairs of sentences. Circle if the second sentence is true or false.

Word Part	Meaning	Examples
cor-	complete; together	correct, corrode
-mit-	send; deliver	submit, emit
-wide	throughout; across	nationwide, citywide

1. The color of the package corresponds to the size of the shirt.
   There's no relationship between the shirt size and the package color. (True / False)

2. The radio tower is on a mountaintop to make it easier to transmit signals.
   The location is designed to improve performance. (True / False)

3. A countywide roadside cleanup effort will take place this Saturday.
   The effort will be carried out all over the county. (True / False)

Grammar *Present Perfect + Passive + Phrasal Verbs*

Phrasal verbs (ex: know about, see to, etc.) are verbs which are followed by prepositions. They are frequently used in the present perfect + passive to indicate completion, usage, or a relationship between things.

Structure: **s + has / have (+ already) + been + pp + preposition**

Ex: The benefits of eating broccoli have been pointed out many times.

Ex: All the banquet preparations have already been seen to.

Complete each sentence using the present perfect + passive. Use the verb in parentheses.

1. The misunderstanding between us _____ (sort out).

2. Due to time conflicts, the meeting _____ (push back) one week.

3. The danger posed by overhanging road signs _____ (bring up) before by city councilors.

4. All of the leakage from the broken pipe _____ (clean up).

Talk About It   Discuss these questions in small groups.

1. The article talks about the color red. Do you wear any special colors or a certain style of clothing when you want to impress someone?

2. What attracts a man to a woman? What are women looking for in men?

3. How do you feel about scientists researching love? Is love possible to understand completely, or will it always remain a mystery?

Write About It

Question: If scientists develop a "love potion" that can make people fall in love, should it be sold in stores? Give two reasons to support your opinion. Prepare by writing notes on the lines below. The first few words of the paragraph are written to help you get started.

Opinion: _____

Reason 1: _____

Reason 2: _____

Selling a love potion in stores would be _____

_____

_____

_____

_____

_____

_____

_____

Listening   Listen to the conversation. Then, answer the following questions.

Track
51

1. (   ) What did the woman do over the weekend?
    (A) She went on a trip.   (B) She worked.
    (C) She rested.   (D) She took a long walk.

2. (   ) What does the man suggest about Parisian neighborhoods?
    (A) They are all full of art galleries.
    (B) A few have nice restaurants.
    (C) Each one has a unique character.
    (D) They are best seen by bicycle.

3. (   ) Where would the woman most like to travel to?
    (A) New York   (B) Paris
    (C) Cincinnati   (D) Moscow

Reading   Read the memo. Then, answer the following questions.

To: All Fillmore Labs Security Personnel   Date: January 29

On January 15, a serious incident occurred with one of the cleaning staff on the 7th floor, where our toxic chemicals division is located. She was cleaning a spilled liquid which turned out to be a strong acid. Unfortunately, she suffered serious burns to her left palm. In response, we're issuing the following guidelines:

1) If you come across any substance on a table or floor, report it to a manager immediately. Do not touch or smell it, even if it looks like water.

2) If you see a bottle or canister nearby, take note of anything written on it, as it may indicate the substance's origin.

3) Do not leave the site until a manager arrives.

1. (   ) What prompted Fillmore Labs to make this announcement?
    (A) A complaint   (B) A lawsuit
    (C) An accident   (D) A survey

2. (   ) What do we learn about the 7th floor?
    (A) People work with hazardous materials there.
    (B) Cleaning staff shouldn't be there after hours.
    (C) Security personnel always guard the floor.
    (D) It has been the site of many serious incidents.

3. (   ) What should a guard do if he or she sees a liquid on the floor?
    (A) Find the cleaning staff   (B) Wipe it up immediately
    (C) Return to the guard office   (D) Inform a supervisor

Supplementary Reading - *Chocolate*

 Track 52

There's no doubting how much we love chocolate. We consume a huge number of chocolate bars, drinks, and bite-sized candies, contributing to an industry worth more than $50 billion in annual sales. What's more, chocolate is widely seen as a "lover's candy," with millions of boxes changing hands on Valentine's Day and other romantic holidays. But what's so special about chocolate, compared to perfectly sensible gifts like a bag of oranges or a subscription to the *Wall Street Journal*? The answer includes an interesting mix of factors.

Marketing is certainly part of the equation. Firms have the presentation of holiday chocolate down to a science, from pink heart-shaped boxes to shiny wrappers for individual pieces. Printed inscriptions like "Be mine" and images of Cupid complete the package. Finally, a pre-Valentine's Day marketing blitz helps convince people that a box of chocolates is just what that special someone needs. For a gift that tastes so good and which can be shared by both people, it's hard to disagree.

Yet chocolate's appeal is not just about fancy sales techniques. Cocoa beans contain a high concentration of phenylethylamine, one of the neurochemicals associated with being in love. Our brain releases the chemical when we're near the object of our affection, making us feel great and focusing our attention on our partner. Holding hands, hugging someone, or just looking into a lover's eyes is all it takes to set off the mental cascade. Therefore, when you give someone chocolate, you really are giving them the candy of love!

Read each sentence. Circle if it is true (T) or false (F).

1. About 50 billion pieces of chocolate are eaten every year.   T / F
2. Shapes and packaging styles are carefully chosen by companies.   T / F
3. Chocolate's popularity is due entirely to good marketing.   T / F
4. When our brain releases phenylethylamine, it helps us concentrate   T / F
   on another person.
5. Phenylethylamine is artificially added to chocolate.   T / F

14 Social Issues

The Homeless

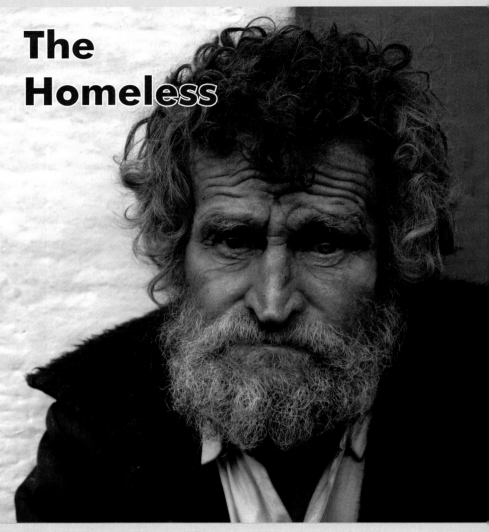

Homelessness is a serious problem in both rich and poor countries. Millions of people have no shelter at all, while many others live in sub-standard housing without running water, sanitation, or electricity. A variety of social and economic factors contribute to the problem.

Pre-Reading Questions Discuss these questions in pairs.

1. Are there many homeless people in your town or city?

2. What do you do when you see a homeless person?

3. What leads to people becoming homeless?

Vocabulary Warmup Track 53

A Listen to the unit's target vocabulary. Then, write the letter of the correct word or phrase next to each definition.

a. abandoned	f. flimsy	k. noble
b. confined to	g. gravity	l. occupant
c. drift	h. grim	m. shelter
d. ensure	i. infrastructure	n. skyrocket
e. feasible	j. latter	o. slum

___ 1. poorly made; weak

___ 2. wander

___ 3. greatly increase at a fast rate

___ 4. person who stays in a place

___ 5. restricted to

___ 6. pure; having good intentions

___ 7. achievable; practical

___ 8. basic facilities such as electricity and running water

___ 9. seriousness

___ 10. make possible; guarantee

B Complete each sentence with a target word or phrase. Remember to use the correct word form.

1. Everyone needs _____ over their heads, especially during the cold winter months.

2. There are two sizes: medium and large. The _____ is big enough for two people to share.

3. After the flood, the situation in the town was _____. Thousands of people needed emergency relief.

4. Since the _____ doesn't have proper sanitation, there's an ongoing risk of water-borne diseases.

5. The street is lined with old _____ cars. The city should have someone tow them away.

Part 1: Reading and Vocabulary Building

1   "Everyone has the right to a standard of living adequate for the health and
    well-being of himself and his family, including food, clothing, housing, and
    medical care..." So reads the UN Declaration of Human Rights, published
    in 1948. Though the goal is **noble**, the reality is **grim**. As the gap between
5   the rich and poor increases, so do poverty and homelessness. The **latter** is a
    complex problem that, according to experts, must be addressed by targeted
    government and community efforts.

    According to UN estimates, there are 100 million people worldwide with no
    shelter whatsoever. These are the visible homeless, sleeping in parks, bus
10 stations, and dark alleys. Yet there are as many as one billion people living
    in inadequate housing. They occupy **abandoned** buildings and crowd into
    slums, sleeping in **flimsy** metal shacks with no running water, sanitation, or
    electricity.

    Sadly, many families and children are among the ranks of the homeless.
15 According to a UN report, there are from 30 to 70 million homeless children
    in Africa and Southeast Asia. Yet the problem isn't **confined to** the developing
    world. In the USA, as many as 3.5 million people experience homelessness at
    some point every year. Of that number, 1.35 million are children.

    A lack of affordable housing is a leading cause of the crisis. Over the last
20 two decades, the cost of living has **skyrocketed** in many cities. In the USA,
    the average rent for a two-bedroom apartment increased 41% from 2000-
    2009. However, wages grew very little during the period. Elsewhere, urban
    development has led to the bulldozing of many low-cost units. For instance,
    from November 2004 to January 2005, 80,000 homes in India were torn down.
25 Most of the 300,000 former **occupants**, with nowhere to go, **drifted** to shanty
    towns. These slums, which circle so many cities, are sad scars created by the
    disparity between the haves and have-nots.

---

⁹ whatsoever – at all
¹² sanitation – series of pipes carrying waste from homes to treatment plants
²³ bulldoze – completely knock down and flatten using heavy machinery
²⁵ shanty town – very poor area made up of shacks

30 Domestic violence is another leading cause of the tragedy. Battered women, fleeing abuse, often have limited or zero financial resources. So, they wind up in shelters or on the street. In Australia, a 2004 survey revealed that of the homeless women aged 25 or older, 43.9% were victims of domestic violence. Besides having nowhere to live, they often suffer from emotional problems, depression, and drug or alcohol abuse.

35 Many other factors contribute to homelessness. People with mental problems and disabilities, inadequately supported by the state, often have trouble paying for housing. Also, people leaving prisons and mental hospitals, as well as those with substance abuse problems, are at risk. The truth is, few people choose to be homeless. Most become so because they literally have nowhere to turn.

40 The best way to help people out of homelessness, while helping prevent the problem in the first place, is to **ensure** an adequate supply of affordable housing. Yet countries often lack the funds or political will to build enough low-cost units.
45 Therefore, some experts suggest that the homeless be allowed "security of tenure" in the shacks that they've built. That means they can continue living there without fear of eviction. If basic **infrastructure**, like water and sanitation, can be added, a slum can
50 be transformed into a healthy community.

Children make up a large percentage of the world's homeless population.

Joining governments in the effort are community groups and non-governmental organizations, which are tackling the crisis one family at a time. Despite the **gravity** of the situation, the UN remains optimistic. One of the goals of the Millennium Summit is to better the living conditions of 100
55 million people in slums. Whether or not that's **feasible** will depend on the ability of governments to adopt creative, long-term solutions to a problem that is all too often ignored.

---

28 domestic – taking place in the home
28 battered – beaten
37 substance abuse – overusing alcohol, drugs, etc.
46 tenure – period of time a person stays or works somewhere
48 eviction – forcing someone to leave a home
52 tackle – take on; deal with

Choose the best answer.

.... **Main Idea**

1. (   ) What is the main idea?
   A. Several factors contribute to the global crisis of homelessness.
   B. The UN has a plan to end homelessness.
   C. It's every person's responsibility to be kind to the homeless.
   D. Many people in India live in shanty towns.

.... **Detail**

2. (   ) Annually, how many American children experience homelessness?
   A. More than one million   B. Roughly 3.5 million
   C. 30 to 70 million   D. About 100 million

.... **Vocabulary**

3. (   ) In line 27, what does "disparity" mean?
   A. misfortune   B. abuse
   C. poverty   D. difference

.... **Analysis**

4. (   ) What can we infer about the UN Declaration of Human Rights?
   A. It was revised during the UN Millennium Summit.
   B. Its hope, as it relates to homelessness, has not yet been realized.
   C. Governments are doing everything they can to support it.
   D. It did not anticipate increases in the cost of living.

5. (   ) Which of the following is NOT a leading cause of homelessness?
   A. Domestic violence against women
   B. Inadequate care for the mentally disabled
   C. An insufficient supply of cheap housing
   D. People choosing to live on the streets

Short Answers   Answer each question based on the article.

1. What basic types of infrastructure are lacking in slums?

   _____

2. Besides homelessness, what issues do victims of domestic violence go through?

   _____

3. What assurance is given to people with security of tenure?

   _____

Vocabulary Building

A Choose the answer that means the same as the word or phrase in italics.

1. The guide says he can *ensure* our safe passage over the mountain pass.
   A. restrict   B. transport   C. promise

2. Unusually cold weather has frozen many crops, sending the price of soybeans *skyrocketing*.
   A. rising   B. planting   C. surviving

3. The *gravity* of the refugee crisis is such that the UN is asking world leaders for emergency aid.
   A. cruelty   B. humanity   C. severity

4. Visitors are *confined to* walking through certain parts of the palace.
   A. attracted to   B. limited to   C. inclined to

5. During serious storms, town residents seek *shelter* in schools and stadiums.
   A. referral   B. protection   C. opportunity

B Complete each sentence with the best word. Remember to use the correct word form.

latter	grim	infrastructure	slum	flimsy

1. You can have green tea or coffee. I'm having the _____.

2. Somewhere around 10,000 people live in the _____, which is located to the northeast of the city.

3. I know things look _____ for the earthquake victims, but trucks carrying aid supplies are on the way.

4. Though it may appear _____, the small plastic table is actually quite strong.

5. Several major _____ projects, including repairing Paddington Bridge, are underway.

C Circle the correct form of each word.

1. The study will determine the (feasible/feasibility) of expanding the reservoir.

2. Offering to give half the proceeds to charity was a (noble/nobility) gesture.

3. (Abandoned/Abandoning) the market doesn't make sense if we still have a loyal customer base.

4. Some (occupants/occupancies) are complaining about the hot water problem.

5. Calvin has spent most of his life (drifts/drifting) from town to town.

Part 2: Focus Areas

Focus on Language

Word Parts

Study the word parts in the chart. Then, read the following pairs of sentences. Circle if the second sentence is true or false.

Word Part	Meaning	Examples
de-	reduce; down	devalue, denounce
-dom-	home	domicile, kingdom
-ible	capable of	flexible, sensible

1. The elevator descends into the mine shaft at a very fast rate.
   People can go down into the mine very quickly. (True / False)

2. In ancient times, a king's power was measured by the size of his domain.
   Personality was the key measurement of a king's power. (True / False)

3. Our eye doctor is famous for his illegible handwriting.
   It's hard to read the doctor's handwriting. (True / False)

Grammar   *Expressions of Quantity + Subject/Verb Agreement*

With expressions of quantity (some of, all of, etc.), the sentence's subject/verb agreement is easily confused. Usually, the verb is based on the noun in the expression of quantity. However, there are exceptions.
Verbs can be singular or plural after: all of, some of, two-thirds of, etc.
Verbs are always singular after: one of, every one of, each of
Ex: Most of the utensils are in the cupboard above the refrigerator.
Ex: One of the teachers was invited to the presidential palace.

Complete each sentence using the verb in parentheses.

1. A lot of sun lovers _____ (go) to the beach every weekend.

2. Every one of the tour buses _____ (be) currently stuck in traffic.

3. Some of the fruit _____ (come) from New Zealand, hence the cost.

4. Each of the employees on the team _____ (work) very hard.

Talk About It   **Discuss these questions in small groups.**

1. In your area, is the cost of living going up? Do you see a rising or falling risk of more people becoming homeless?

2. How does your town or city deal with its homeless situation?

3. Why is it that, even in rich countries, there are many homeless people?

Write About It

Question: Do you agree or disagree with granting homeless people "security of tenure" in the shacks that they've built? Give two reasons to support your opinion. Prepare by writing notes on the lines below. The first few words of the paragraph are written to help you get started.

Opinion: _____

Reason 1: _____

Reason 2: _____

The practice of security of tenure is, in my opinion, _____

_____

_____

_____

_____

_____

_____

_____

_____

Listening   **Listen to the report. Then, answer the following questions.**

Track 55

1. (   ) How far from Guatemala City was the quake's epicenter?
   (A) 200 kilometers
   (B) 700 kilometers
   (C) 1,100 kilometers
   (D) 1,950 kilometers

2. (   ) Why have many people gone to Olympic City?
   (A) To obey a government order
   (B) To watch a special event
   (C) To look for protection
   (D) To search for their relatives

3. (   ) Who will assist the government in its rescue efforts?
   (A) The United Nations
   (B) The people in Olympic City
   (C) The city officials
   (D) The national army

Reading   **Choose the correct word(s) to fill in each blank.**

As downtown rental prices skyrocket, people are taking drastic measures to make ends meet. One trend is for people to move to suburbs 60-90 minutes away from the city. However, that's (___1___) long commute, and high gas prices mean the option is only feasible for commuters who own a fuel-efficient vehicle. Some people are opting to stay in tiny rooms during the week, (___2___) home only on weekends and holidays. In a sign of the gravity of many workers' situations, a growing number are sleeping in their cars several nights per week. The city has even set up designated "Car Ports" (___3___) people may legally (and safely) sleep in their vehicles.

1. (   ) (A) such   (B) too
        (C) a   (D) the

2. (   ) (A) return   (B) returned
        (C) returning   (D) will return

3. (   ) (A) which   (B) where
        (C) what   (D) whom

Supplementary Reading - *The Homeless World Cup* Track 56

The power of sport is amazing. Aside from being great exercise, it brings people together as they rally behind local and national teams. Sport can also engender social change. That's the goal of the Homeless World Cup, an annual event that helps homeless people better their lives through playing one of the world's most popular sports: soccer.

The Homeless World Cup is overseen by organizers in Edinburgh, Scotland. The event was first held in Graz, Austria in 2003, with players from five countries participating. Since then, it has been hosted by cities in Africa, Australia, and South America. Thanks in part to great media coverage, the event's size and popularity have rapidly grown. In 2008, when Melbourne, Australia was the host city, athletes from 56 countries participated, with 100,000 spectators cheering them on.

Organizers are proud of the tournament's solid outcomes. As part of the yearly selection process, some 25,000 homeless people are involved in training programs. The activity provides them with a sense of purpose. Those who make the national teams show measurable progress in their lives. For instance, after the 2005 Cup in Edinburgh, 12 athletes joined professional or semi-professional soccer teams. After the 2006 Cup in Cape Town, South Africa, a solid 73% of participants went on to better themselves by finding work, moving into permanent housing, going back to school, and/or getting treatment for drug or alcohol addiction. What's more, a full 92% of participants that year said the experience improved their outlook on life.

Read each sentence. Circle if it is true (T) or false (F).

1. The Homeless World Cup has been held on four continents. T / F
2. From 2003 to 2008, the number of participating countries grew from 5 to 56. T / F
3. About 100,000 athletes take part in the yearly event. T / F
4. Being part of the training process can benefit homeless people. T / F
5. Following the Cape Town tournament, 12 homeless people joined professional teams. T / F

15 Globalization

Is the world ready for a single currency?

In the global economy, more than a trillion US dollars worth of currencies are bought and sold every day. This enormous currency flow involves risks like exchange rate instability and currency speculation. Some people think we could solve these problems by creating a single world currency.

Pre-Reading Questions   Discuss these questions in pairs.

1. What are some of the world's major currencies?

2. How can currency exchange rates hurt people and businesses?

3. Is the world ready for a single global currency (which could be used in every country)? Why or why not?

Vocabulary Warmup Track 57

A **Listen to the unit's target vocabulary. Then, write the letter of the correct word or phrase next to each definition.**

a. appreciate	f. crippling	k. road block
b. astounding	g. expose	l. shudder
c. chorus of voices	h. first and foremost	m. stabilize
d. commodity	i. mastermind	n. underscore
e. consensus	j. proposal	o. wipe the slate clean

___ 1. obstacle

___ 2. amazing

___ 3. suggestion; offer

___ 4. highlight; emphasize

___ 5. agreement

___ 6. very damaging

___ 7. rise in value

___ 8. item; product

___ 9. direct; oversee

___ 10. most importantly

B **Complete each sentence with a target word or phrase. Remember to use the correct word form.**

1. After weeks of wild price swings, the stock market is starting to _____. Prices haven't moved much today.

2. A large _____ is backing the new highway. Fifty thousand people have signed a petition for its construction.

3. Upgrading the old software would take too much time and money. Let's _____ and design a new system.

4. I _____ when I heard electricity prices would be rising again.

5. Investing in commercial real estate will _____ us to property value risks.

Part 1: Reading and Vocabulary Building

1   In our interconnected world, we buy, sell, trade, and lend to each other on an unprecedented scale. Every day, some $1.4 trillion worth of currencies is exchanged, driving global trade and finance. Yet the current system, which consists of some 190 currencies, possesses a high degree of instability, posing
5   risks to businesses and nations. In response, a growing **chorus of voices** is calling for the creation of a single global currency. Critics of the idea say the time isn't right to overhaul the way we do business.

Currently, international business is largely conducted in US dollars. Also, contracts for oil, corn, wheat, and other **commodities** are typically
10   denominated in the currency. However, this system **exposes** companies to significant risks. If their local currency falls against the greenback, it makes imports more expensive. And, when a nation's currency **appreciates**, it makes exports more costly while threatening profits. Executives at Toyota, Mercedes, and Airbus SAS **shudder** when their local currencies become too
15   strong.

On the national level, the stakes are even higher, as central banks hold massive foreign currency reserves. Countries maintain reserves to boost their credit worthiness and protect the local currency from sudden drops in value. As of October 2009, total worldwide reserves stood at $7.3 trillion, an
20   **astounding** increase from the 1999 total of $1.7 trillion. China leads the way, with foreign assets of more than $2.1 trillion.

As electronic commerce allows vast sums to change hands, fluctuations in domestic and reserve currencies can be swift and violent. The 1997 Asian financial crisis saw a variety of currencies come under attack, severely
25   damaging local economies. Other crises in Mexico, Russia, and elsewhere have **underscored** the **crippling** impact of currency crises. Likewise, when the value of a reserve currency falls, nations can suffer huge losses.

---

7 overhaul – completely change or reform
10 denominated in – based on a certain currency
11 greenback – US dollar
22 fluctuation – upward or downward change

In response to this instability, a growing number of countries want to **wipe the slate clean** and put a single currency in place. Nations including China, Russia, India, and South Korea feel a global currency would **stabilize** financial markets while finally putting speculators out of business. A single currency would also reduce waste, as some $400 billion a year is spent on currency exchange fees. Among the supporters are prominent economists like Robert Mundell, the Nobel laureate who **masterminded** Europe's transition to the euro. Another backer is the Single Global Currency Association, which hopes to see a global currency in place by 2025.

Despite the attractiveness of the **proposal**, some important concerns remain. **First and foremost** is the question of control. A global currency would be overseen by a new Global Central Bank, which would possess tools to direct monetary policy. However, that would present individual countries, no longer in possession of such tools, with a harder time steering their economies through rough patches. Furthermore, as countries have diverse economic and political systems, it might be hard to reach **consensus** on the details of a global system. Finally, nations have historic ties to their currencies, which their citizens may not easily give up. As the former Bank of America president put it, "The control of money and credit strikes at the very heart of national sovereignty."

A single currency would end exchange rate instability and speculation.

Despite these **road blocks**, there are already regional examples of currency consolidation in place. The euro has helped integrate the European market, while in the Caribbean, the East Caribbean dollar is used by eight political states. Plans for future regional currencies exist in Asia and elsewhere. Yet for now, the US dollar, along with the euro and yen, still dominate global commerce. Will these juggernauts be replaced by a single global currency? In some people's minds, it's not a question of if that will happen, but when.

---

[31] speculator – investor looking for a quick rise in value
[34] Nobel laureate – Nobel prize winner
[35] transition – switch over
[40] monetary policy – rules directing a currency's interest rates, supply, etc.
[43] rough patch – difficult period
[50] sovereignty – self-government by a nation

Choose the best answer.

.... **Main Idea**

1. (   ) What is the main idea?
    A. A single global currency will be in place by 2025.
    B. The idea of a global currency has plenty of support and criticism.
    C. Imports and exports are both affected by currency swings.
    D. Currency reform is one of many moves needed to stabilize world trade.

.... **Detail**

2. (   ) What happened to the world's currency reserves from 1999 to 2009?
    A. They increased by more than $5 trillion.
    B. They fell to a total of $2.1 trillion.
    C. They rose to a national average of $7.3 trillion.
    D. They went up by $1.7 trillion per year.

.... **Vocabulary**

3. (   ) In line 43, what does "steering" mean?
    A. directing   B. possessing
    C. investing   D. expanding

.... **Analysis**

4. (   ) What does the article imply about monetary policy tools?
    A. A Global Central Bank would rarely need them.
    B. Countries will still use them after a single global currency is in place.
    C. They make it more difficult for economies to survive hard times.
    D. Nations may be reluctant to give them up.

5. (   ) Which of these advantages of a single global currency is NOT discussed?
    A. An opportunity for increased international trade
    B. Money saved on foreign exchange fees
    C. An end to speculation and currency crises
    D. Stabilization of the global financial system

Short Answers   **Answer each question based on the article.**

1. How are commodity imports affected when the local currency falls?

_____

2. Why do countries keep large foreign currency reserves?

_____

3. What are two regional currencies which are currently in use?

_____

Vocabulary Building

A **Choose the answer that means the same as the word or phrase in italics.**

1. Half the friends want to travel to Singapore, but the other half prefer Hong Kong. They're having trouble reaching a *consensus*.
   A. itinerary   B. agreement   C. debate

2. With so many people out of work, when is the economy going to *stabilize*?
   A. settle down   B. shoot up   C. look back

3. In the past, *commodities* like silk were highly valued in Europe.
   A. products   B. threads   C. nations

4. The roommates, who had often quarreled, agreed to *wipe the slate clean* and try to get along.
   A. assign fault   B. act fairly   C. start anew

5. *First and foremost*, I'd like to thank everyone for their hard work.
   A. In conclusion   B. Above all   C. With sincerity

B **Complete each sentence with the best word or phrase. Remember to use the correct word form.**

> mastermind   road block   underscore   shudder   chorus of voices

1. The Committee to Save the Old Courthouse has encountered a serious _____, but they're still confident they will succeed.

2. It's been so cold, I _____ to think of our next heating bill.

3. The ad campaign was _____ by our top strategist.

4. There's a large _____ calling for more art classes in elementary schools.

5. The string of accidents at the intersection _____ the need for a traffic light there.

C **Circle the correct form of each word.**

1. The power plant engineer was rewarded for (expose/exposing) weaknesses in the design.

2. We'll need one or two weeks to review your (proposal/propose).

3. After visiting the weather bureau, the 5th grade class wrote a letter to express their (appreciate/appreciation).

4. Losing a major client can be (crippling/crippled) to a small firm.

5. There are an (astounded/astounding) number of entertainment choices in a city like Tokyo.

Focus on Language

Word Parts

Study the word parts in the chart. Then, read the following pairs of sentences. Circle if the second sentence is true or false.

Word Part	Meaning	Examples
over-	above; beyond	oversee, overcharge
-sen(s)-	feeling	consent, sensory
-or	performer of an action	investor, surveyor

1. Mr. Morris said he was willing to overlook Lauren's mistake.
   Lauren will not be punished for her error. (True / False)

2. The general sentiment is, by working together, we can stop global warming.
   Few people feel there's anything we can do about the problem. (True / False)

3. During the match, the spectators cheered Ronaldo's ball-handling skill.
   Ronaldo's teammates made a lot of noise. (True / False)

Grammar — *It's not a question of...*

This structure is used to negate one thing while emphasizing another. The sentence's first idea is negated or considered unimportant. The second idea is the key point.
Structure: **It's not a question of + (word, phrase, or clause), but (of) + (word, phrase, or clause)**
Ex: It's not a question of price, but of quality.
Ex: It's not a question of if we will win, but by how many points.

Combine the two sentences using *it's not a question of...*

1. We don't care about the taste. We care about the nutritional quality.

   _____

2. Whether he'll go to college isn't the issue. Where he'll go is the question.

   _____

3. What she will say isn't so important. To whom she will say it is.

   _____

Talk About It   Discuss these questions in small groups.

1. In the global financial system, a few major currencies dominate international trade. Is this a good thing, a bad thing, or both?

2. A single global currency will require extensive cooperation between countries. Can countries put their differences aside and make that happen?

3. What do you think about creating new regional currencies (such as an Asia-wide currency) before a single global currency is put in place?

Write About It

Question: Will the world see a single global currency within 20 years? Give two reasons to support your opinion. Prepare by writing notes on the lines below. The first few words of the paragraph are written to help you get started.

Opinion: _____

Reason 1: _____

Reason 2: _____

Twenty years from now, the world _____

_____

_____

_____

_____

_____

_____

_____

Listening

Listen to the conversation. Then, answer the following questions.

🔘 Track 59

1. (   ) What kind of company do they work for?
   (A) An exchange bank   (B) A parts supplier
   (C) A components designer   (D) An investment firm

2. (   ) What happened to the euro last month?
   (A) It rose 4% against the Korean won.
   (B) It rose 2% against the US dollar.
   (C) It fell 15% against the Korean won.
   (D) It fell 0.5% against the US dollar.

3. (   ) What does the man suggest about the next quarterly report?
   (A) The report will be very bad.
   (B) There will be no excuse for its results.
   (C) It's going to impress the board.
   (D) It will beat their Korean competitors.

Reading

Read the letter. Then, answer the following questions.

Dear Ms. McLeary,

Thank you for your proposal to write a guide book on Russia. We actually have one in development, and it will go to press in six months. Something we do need is a Russian/English phrase book. Your advanced degree in Russian studies makes you an excellent candidate for the task. If that interests you, let me know, and I'll send you our phrase title guidelines. If you could also put together three pages on "Russian for Dining Out," that would be helpful. First and foremost, I need to underscore that we'd like to get this out by year's end. So please get back to me as soon as possible.

Best regards,

Reginald Pullman

1. (   ) What does the company currently need?
   (A) A Russia guide book   (B) A collection of stories
   (C) A new catalogue   (D) A Russian phrase book

2. (   ) What makes Ms. McLeary qualified for the proposed task?
   (A) Her traveling experience   (B) Her writing history
   (C) Her educational background   (D) Her translator credentials

3. (   ) What does Mr. Pullman want her to do?
   (A) Send him a set of guidelines   (B) Write some sample material
   (C) Attend a dinner party   (D) Finish the task by next year

Supplementary Reading - *The Euro*

 Track 60

Proponents of a global currency point to the euro as a shining example of the benefits of currency consolidation. The long road to the euro dates back to 1957, when the European Union was formed to improve economic integration between member states. Over time, this has been accomplished through the lowering of trade barriers, establishment of a single market for goods and labor, and, eventually, the creation of a single currency.

The euro was launched in 1999, first as a "virtual" currency for bank wires and other non-cash transactions. Then, in 2002, euro notes and coins were issued. Over time, the number of EU members who adopted the euro (and gave up their national currencies) grew from 11 to 16. Several others, including Poland and Romania, are taking steps to add to this total. Yet not all  EU countries are interested in being part of the "euro zone." Both the UK and Denmark have chosen to retain their national currencies.

Some 329 million people in the euro zone use the currency on a daily basis. Using a single currency lets them realize many benefits, including price stability and transparency. Consumers and businesspeople in the euro zone can easily compare prices for goods and services, facilitating economic growth and cooperation. The euro also helps protect member countries from raw material and energy price fluctuations. On the global stage, the euro is already the world's second-most traded currency (behind the US dollar). It's widely used to conduct international transactions and is an important national reserve currency.

Read each sentence. Circle if it is true (T) or false (F).

1. The euro was launched before trade barriers were lowered in the EU. T / F
2. It took several years for the euro to transition from a virtual to a cash-based currency. T / F
3. The euro zone includes all EU member countries. T / F
4. Denmark is taking steps to adopt the euro and give up its national currency. T / F
5. Outside the EU, the euro is important in international trade. T / F

16

The Future of Humanity

New technologies are having a stronger and stronger impact on our lives. Medical advances may, within decades, greatly lengthen our life spans. Other developments in genetics, robotics, and space travel could profoundly change our basic concepts of humanity.

Pre-Reading Questions   Discuss these questions in pairs.

1. In general, are you optimistic or pessimistic about the future?

2. In the future, will the gap between the rich and poor continue to grow?

3. Do you think people will be very different 100 years from now? If so, how?

Vocabulary Warmup Track 61

A **Listen to the unit's target vocabulary. Then, write the letter of the correct word next to each definition.**

a. attribute	f. institution	k. salient
b. civilization	g. interface	l. scenario
c. diverge	h. lingering	m. stockpile
d. dwindle	i. marvel	n. undoing
e. implication	j. radical	o. unleash

___ 1. situation; set of circumstances

___ 2. supply; store

___ 3. characteristic

___ 4. release; let loose

___ 5. downfall; ruin

___ 6. greatly decrease

___ 7. split; go in different directions

___ 8. organization

___ 9. consequence; effect

___ 10. wonder; sensation

B **Complete each sentence with a target word. Remember to use the correct word form.**

1. One of the most _____ arguments against the new stadium is the lack of funds to pay for it.

2. The ancient Egyptian _____ is known for its massive building projects, such as the Sphinx and the pyramids.

3. The oil spill has been cleaned up, but there are _____ effects, such as the lack of wildlife in the area.

4. A bank machine's _____ must be clear and simple so anybody can figure it out.

5. Successful recycling programs can lead to a(n) _____ decrease in garbage levels.

Part 1: Reading and Vocabulary Building

1   In our world of technological **marvels** and medical breakthroughs, it's easy to
forget that **civilization** is only 10,000 years old. Indeed, in the last 100 years,
we've discovered and invented more than in all of human history combined.
Yet this is just the beginning. Within the next few centuries, technology could
5   bring **radical** shifts in what it means to be human. The coming evolutionary
leap has some hopeful and others worried.

Many futurists feel the first step will be an extension of our life spans.
Currently, the average life expectancy is 77 years, but medical research could,
within decades, push that to 120. Through genetic manipulation, scientists
10   have greatly expanded the life spans of small animals like mice. For instance,
work at the University of California, San Francisco has led to the doubling
of the life spans of round worms. Nanotechnology may also play a key role.
Author Raymond Kurzweil feels that by 2029, we could have nanomachines
coursing through our bodies, fighting off infections at the cellular level.

15   Over the long term, genetic procedures could change our most basic features.
Through "reprogenetics," parents may one day order "upgrade packages"
for their unborn children, allowing them to grow up stronger, smarter,
and more attractive. Such **attributes** will be passed on from generation to
generation, initiating a form of rapid evolution. This worries futurists like
20   Oliver Curry, an evolutionary theorist at the London School of Economics.
Since the greatest advantages will be enjoyed by the wealthy, he suggests
the human race could **diverge** into two distinct sub-species: an upperclass
and an underclass. Such a shift would have profound social and economic
implications.

25   Other visions of the future see a closer integration of humans and machines.
We already enhance our natural skills through artificial networks like the
Internet. It's possible that within a few centuries, people could physically

[16] reprogenetics – combination of the words "reproduction" and "genetics"

30 "plug into" machines. Futurist Vernor Vinge calls this type of human/machine **interface** "intelligence amplification." It could allow us to access data and control machines with our thoughts, providing fantastic creative opportunities. Some scientists even suggest that in the future, we'll transfer our minds into artificial bodies, allowing us to live forever.

35 Looking further downfield, some feel space exploration is our common destiny. As the Earth's population grows while its resources **dwindle**, we may eventually be forced to survive by living on other planets. Renowned scientist Stephen Hawking suggests the moon or Mars could be prime locations for colonies. In his words, "I believe the long-term future of the human race must be in space."

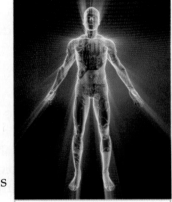

40 As exciting as these visions are, there's ample concern that things won't turn out so well. A recent UN report entitled the "Global Environment Outlook" warns that crises such as global warming and overdevelopment have placed us on a path of environmental ruin. Others fear that technology, rather than enriching our lives, might be our

45 **undoing**. Bio-terrorists could **unleash** deadly viruses affecting entire populations. Furthermore, there's **lingering** concern that the world's **stockpile** of nuclear weapons could trigger a devastating war.

Human/machine interfaces could greatly enhance many of our skills.

50 Whichever path we take, the future is fast approaching. Within 50 years, longer life spans and new discoveries could change many of our **institutions**, values, and core beliefs. As we peer ahead into the distance, perhaps the most **salient** course will be to take a hard look at all the options. In his book *Radical Evolution*, futurist Joel Garreau lays out multiple **scenarios** for the future.

55 Some, like the Heaven scenario, paint an optimistic picture. Others, like the Hell scenario, are just the opposite. Individually and collectively, as people and as a species, the choices we make will determine the path we pursue.

---

33 further downfield – further into the future
35 renowned – famous
46 bio-terrorist – terrorist who uses biological weapons

Choose the best answer.

.... **Main Idea**

1. (   ) What is the main idea?
   A. Mankind faces a range of possible future paths.
   B. Our future will be decided by the wealthiest people.
   C. It's easy to determine where the human race is headed.
   D. Machines will soon play an even bigger role in our lives.

.... **Detail**

2. (   ) Which scholar is concerned about a human evolutionary split?
   A. Stephen Hawking   B. Vernor Vinge
   C. Raymond Kurzweil   D. Oliver Curry

.... **Vocabulary**

3. (   ) In line 19, what does "initiating" mean?
   A. replacing   B. applauding
   C. gathering   D. introducing

.... **Analysis**

4. (   ) According to the article, what worries the UN?
   A. They fear we are causing severe damage to the environment.
   B. They are deeply concerned about nuclear weapons.
   C. They worry bio-terrorists are preparing to launch an attack.
   D. They believe most people have a negative outlook.

5. (   ) How would people benefit from "intelligence amplification"?
   A. By being cured of most illnesses by nanomachines
   B. By inheriting a better set of genes from their parents
   C. By enjoying enhancements of their creative potential
   D. By getting data from traditional sources like libraries

Short Answers   Answer each question based on the article.

1. What does the article suggest about the future of human life spans?

_____

2. What advantage would be gained by transferring our minds into machines?

_____

3. In the future, why may people need to live on other planets?

_____

Vocabulary Building

Ⓐ Choose the answer that means the same as the word in italics.

1. After its completion, the Empire State Building was considered a *marvel* of the world.
   A. celebration   B. wonder   C. jealousy

2. One of the *implications* of higher food prices is fewer people are eating out.
   A. supports   B. industries   C. consequences

3. Athletes sometimes feel the *lingering* effects of their injuries for years.
   A. financial   B. painful   C. remaining

4. For emergencies, we keep a small *stockpile* of canned food in the basement.
   A. supply   B. recipe   C. nutrition

5. I can think of a few *scenarios* which would make me want to move to another place.
   A. neighbors   B. circumstances   C. compliments

Ⓑ Complete each sentence with the best word. Remember to use the correct word form.

undoing	civilization	interface	unleash	salient

1. This control _____ can be operated with just one hand.

2. Astor brought up some _____ points about the need for better security.

3. I doubt the new coffee shop next door will be our _____, but it certainly won't help either.

4. The Chinese _____ can be traced back thousands of years.

5. Global warming, if it continues at the present rate, could _____ huge typhoons on a regular basis.

Ⓒ Circle the correct form of each word.

1. One way to keep our raw materials from (dwindle/dwindling) too quickly is by consuming less.

2. By installing solar panels, the Johnsons have (radically/radical) lowered their energy bills.

3. Loyalty, friendliness, and attention to detail are some of the most prized (attributes/attributed) in an employee.

4. The road (diverges/divergence) up ahead, after another two miles.

5. (Institution/Institutional) borrowing by large firms is up five percent.

Part 2: Focus Areas

Focus on Language

Word Parts

Study the word parts in the chart. Then, read the following pairs of sentences. Circle if the second sentence is true or false.

Word Part	Meaning	Examples
multi-	many	multitask, multiply
-gen-	live; create	progeny, gender
-ist	believer; performer	machinist, violinist

1. The famine in West Africa has prompted a multinational relief effort.
   A number of countries will be involved in the operation. (True / False)

2. We have an electric generator which we use during power outages.
   The machine is used when the normal power supply is interrupted. (True / False)

3. Once a month, the columnist writes about an aspect of city life.
   The articles appear in print 12 times per year. (True / False)

Grammar   *By + future vs. By + future perfect*

Use "by + future tense" to say that by a certain future time, something will happen. To say that by a certain future time, something will be completed, use "by + future perfect."

Structure: **(future): By + time/date, s + will + original verb**
            (future perfect): By + time/date, s + will have + pp

Ex: By the year 2100, people will live in underwater cities.

Ex: By 2050, we will have cured most types of cancer.

Using the information, write a sentence about the future.

1. **Time**: 2075   **Action**: own flying cars   **Tense**: future

   _____

2. **Time**: 22nd century   **Action**: end world hunger   **Tense**: future perfect

   _____

3. **Time**: 2300   **Action**: make contact with aliens   **Tense**: future perfect

   _____

Talk About It   Discuss these questions in small groups.

1. If you could have your children's DNA altered so that they're born taller, stronger, or more attractive, would you do it? Why or why not?

2. How about plugging into a machine body, with a chance to live forever? Does that appeal to you?

3. Environmental concerns top many people's worries about the future. Will humanity solve these problems before it's too late?

Write About It

Question: Technologies like reprogenetics will likely be expensive. Is it fair that the rich will have first access to them? Give two reasons to support your opinion. Prepare by writing notes on the lines below. The first few words of the paragraph are written to help you get started.

Opinion: _____

Reason 1: _____

Reason 2: _____

In the future, advanced technologies

Listening   **Listen to the speech. Then, answer the following questions.**

Track
63

1. (   ) What is the woman's likely occupation?
        (A) Stockbroker   (B) Tour guide
        (C) City official   (D) Financial analyst

2. (   ) What greatly changed the New York Stock Exchange?
        (A) Government regulation
        (B) Hollywood movies
        (C) Overseas cooperation
        (D) Electronic trading

3. (   ) What does the woman suggest about the NYSE?
        (A) It only deals with US stocks.
        (B) It handles billions of transactions.
        (C) It is quiet most of the time.
        (D) It has resisted modernizing.

Reading   **Choose the correct word(s) to fill in each blank.**

This June, an extraordinary meeting of world leaders (___1___) in Geneva. The so-called Civilization Quorum will bring together 150 presidents, prime ministers, and monarchs. They'll be joined by leading academics and scientists. The Quorum will identify the 10 greatest achievements of the world's civilizations, as well as our 10 greatest challenges. Special attention will be placed on environmental issues such as global warming and our dwindling natural resources. According to a survey (___2___) 20 million people, the environment tops people's lists of concerns. The implications of the Quorum's conclusions could be profound, as they'll help shape (___3___) countries' policies as well as those of the United Nations and other global organizations.

1. (   ) (A) is holding   (B) being held
      (C) will be held   (D) to hold

2. (   ) (A) distributed to   (B) substituted for
      (C) referred by   (D) withdrawn from

3. (   ) (A) individually   (B) individual
      (C) individualize   (D) individualism

Supplementary Reading - *The City of the Future*   Track 64

In the future, the places we inhabit will help shape who we become. Some futurists envision urban landscapes full of flying cars, moveable sidewalks, and intelligent robots. Yet those visions tend to have unclear timeframes, resting somewhere in the mid to distant future. Masdar City, in contrast, is one country's attempt to build the city of the future today. Powered by renewable energy sources, Masdar will be the world's cleanest city.

Masdar is being built in Abu Dhabi, the largest member of the UAE. The city, whose $22 billion construction cost is being funded by a government-backed initiative, will occupy a six-square kilometer patch of desert. Eventually, it will house some 50,000 residents, more than 1,500 businesses, and a university.

Masdar City's key feature will be its sustainability. Buildings will be fully powered by solar and wind power, and water will be provided by a solar-powered desalination plant. Nearly all the city's waste, including run-off water from surrounding farms, will be recycled. Instead of driving cars, people will get around via an underground Personal Rapid Transit system. Small electric vehicles will take passengers to one of around 1,500 stations.

Abu Dhabi hopes to use Masdar City to develop and test clean energy technologies in a real-world setting. Though the emirate has made its fortune from its rich oil reserves, it wants to position itself as a leader in 21st century clean industries. The world will be watching as Abu Dhabi's cutting edge city of the future takes shape.

Read each sentence. Circle if it is true (T) or false (F).

1. Masdar City will have approximately 1,500 residents.   T / F
2. The city will be modeled after other cities in the UAE.   T / F
3. Electricity in Masdar City will come from renewable power sources.   T / F
4. Great effort will be put into recycling the city's waste.   T / F
5. Masdar City is part of Abu Dhabi's long-term economic plan.   T / F

Target Vocabulary List

☐ abandoned	Unit 14		☐ chorus of voices	Unit 15
☐ acclimatize	Unit 10		☐ civilization	Unit 16
☐ accomplish	Unit 11		☐ coin (a term)	Unit 6
☐ activate	Unit 13		☐ coincide with	Unit 4
☐ adequate	Unit 9		☐ coincidence	Unit 5
☐ aesthetic	Unit 1		☐ collectively	Unit 4
☐ allergic	Unit 7		☐ collide	Unit 12
☐ ample	Unit 2		☐ commodity	Unit 15
☐ anthropologist	Unit 10		☐ compel	Unit 3
☐ appliance	Unit 4		☐ compound	Unit 10
☐ appreciate	Unit 15		☐ concerted	Unit 3
☐ appropriate	Unit 11		☐ conduct	Unit 5
☐ arise	Unit 9		☐ confined to	Unit 14
☐ astounding	Unit 15		☐ conflict	Unit 10
☐ at (something's) core	Unit 3		☐ connoisseur	Unit 8
☐ attribute	Unit 16		☐ conscious	Unit 11
☐ avatar	Unit 5		☐ consensus	Unit 15
☐ befriend	Unit 10		☐ constructive	Unit 4
☐ biotech	Unit 7		☐ contribution	Unit 4
☐ bluntly	Unit 6		☐ counseling	Unit 3
☐ boast	Unit 8		☐ crawl	Unit 11
☐ bombard	Unit 9		☐ crippling	Unit 15
☐ boost	Unit 7		☐ criticism	Unit 11
☐ brainstorm	Unit 2		☐ daunting	Unit 9
☐ broaden (one's) horizons	Unit 10		☐ dedication	Unit 2
☐ cash in on	Unit 6		☐ devoted to	Unit 7
☐ catastrophe	Unit 12		☐ dialogue	Unit 10
☐ certified	Unit 1		☐ discipline	Unit 8
☐ chamber	Unit 9		☐ dispatch	Unit 12
☐ child rearing	Unit 3		☐ disposable income	Unit 6

☐ diverge	Unit 16		☐ flimsy	Unit 14
☐ drawback	Unit 3		☐ flourish	Unit 8
☐ drift	Unit 14		☐ from the outset	Unit 4
☐ drought	Unit 7		☐ genetics	Unit 7
☐ dwindle	Unit 16		☐ get into the act	Unit 8
☐ elated	Unit 13		☐ gravity	Unit 14
☐ element	Unit 10		☐ grim	Unit 14
☐ elevated	Unit 13		☐ harsh	Unit 7
☐ embark	Unit 9		☐ harvest	Unit 4
☐ empathetic	Unit 1		☐ hijack	Unit 12
☐ encounter	Unit 2		☐ hormone	Unit 13
☐ endangered	Unit 4		☐ hostile	Unit 2
☐ endorsement	Unit 8		☐ ignore	Unit 6
☐ enhance	Unit 5		☐ illustrate	Unit 5
☐ ensure	Unit 14		☐ immune to	Unit 3
☐ envelop	Unit 5		☐ implication	Unit 16
☐ equipped with	Unit 2		☐ in essence	Unit 1
☐ evolve	Unit 1		☐ in the face of	Unit 4
☐ expatriate	Unit 3		☐ incident	Unit 12
☐ expose	Unit 15		☐ indicate	Unit 13
☐ extension	Unit 5		☐ indulge	Unit 6
☐ facet	Unit 5		☐ inevitably	Unit 10
☐ facilitate	Unit 1		☐ infant	Unit 8
☐ fascinating	Unit 13		☐ infrastructure	Unit 14
☐ feasible	Unit 14		☐ initially	Unit 3
☐ fickle	Unit 5		☐ inject	Unit 2
☐ figure of speech	Unit 13		☐ insight	Unit 1
☐ first and foremost	Unit 15		☐ inspiration	Unit 1
☐ fixate	Unit 13		☐ instantly	Unit 13
☐ fleeting	Unit 8		☐ institution	Unit 16

☐ interface	Unit 16	☐ organism	Unit 7
☐ interrupt	Unit 11	☐ out of favor	Unit 5
☐ introverted	Unit 10	☐ outsmart	Unit 2
☐ juggernaut	Unit 8	☐ oxygen	Unit 9
☐ justification	Unit 7	☐ palm	Unit 13
☐ latter	Unit 14	☐ paramount	Unit 10
☐ legislation	Unit 4	☐ passion	Unit 13
☐ legitimate	Unit 7	☐ patent	Unit 7
☐ lethal	Unit 12	☐ peer	Unit 9
☐ leverage	Unit 8	☐ per capita	Unit 3
☐ lingering	Unit 16	☐ perspective	Unit 10
☐ linguistic	Unit 3	☐ pesticide	Unit 7
☐ lucrative	Unit 8	☐ pioneer	Unit 9
☐ manipulate	Unit 7	☐ politician	Unit 4
☐ marvel	Unit 16	☐ port	Unit 12
☐ mastermind	Unit 15	☐ potion	Unit 13
☐ mature	Unit 6	☐ precedent	Unit 2
☐ menacing	Unit 9	☐ precision	Unit 11
☐ merchant	Unit 12	☐ prerequisite	Unit 1
☐ microscopic	Unit 2	☐ proficient	Unit 11
☐ mindset	Unit 6	☐ profoundly	Unit 2
☐ monopoly	Unit 7	☐ prominence	Unit 13
☐ motive	Unit 12	☐ prone to	Unit 12
☐ nexus	Unit 2	☐ proposal	Unit 15
☐ noble	Unit 14	☐ pros and cons	Unit 6
☐ nurturing	Unit 13	☐ provoke	Unit 12
☐ obtain	Unit 1	☐ pulse	Unit 11
☐ occupant	Unit 14	☐ radiation	Unit 9
☐ opt	Unit 6	☐ radical	Unit 16
☐ orbit	Unit 9	☐ ramification	Unit 6

☐ ransom	Unit 12		☐ substance	Unit 13
☐ remarkable	Unit 6		☐ sympathetic	Unit 10
☐ replicate	Unit 2		☐ take heart	Unit 6
☐ resolve	Unit 11		☐ take root	Unit 4
☐ restraint	Unit 5		☐ tangible	Unit 1
☐ retrieve	Unit 9		☐ teleportation	Unit 2
☐ revive	Unit 9		☐ tense up	Unit 11
☐ rhythm	Unit 11		☐ the lion's share	Unit 12
☐ road block	Unit 15		☐ therapeutic	Unit 1
☐ salient	Unit 16		☐ thermal	Unit 2
☐ savvy	Unit 8		☐ toil	Unit 3
☐ scenario	Unit 16		☐ transform	Unit 8
☐ self-esteem	Unit 1		☐ trigger	Unit 11
☐ sheer	Unit 5		☐ underlying	Unit 3
☐ shelter	Unit 14		☐ underscore	Unit 15
☐ shudder	Unit 15		☐ undoing	Unit 16
☐ skyrocket	Unit 14		☐ unforeseen	Unit 7
☐ slum	Unit 14		☐ unleash	Unit 16
☐ slump	Unit 11		☐ unscrupulous	Unit 3
☐ socialize	Unit 5		☐ urbanization	Unit 4
☐ spearhead	Unit 4		☐ utmost	Unit 11
☐ speculation	Unit 9		☐ venue	Unit 5
☐ springboard	Unit 1		☐ verbalize	Unit 1
☐ sputter	Unit 3		☐ vice-versa	Unit 10
☐ stabilize	Unit 15		☐ vital	Unit 4
☐ stake (one's) claim	Unit 5		☐ vulnerable	Unit 12
☐ stay put	Unit 6		☐ walk of life	Unit 8
☐ steady	Unit 6		☐ ward off	Unit 12
☐ stereotype	Unit 10		☐ wipe the slate clean	Unit 15
☐ stockpile	Unit 16		☐ woo	Unit 8

About the Author

Andrew E. Bennett holds an EdM (Master of Education) degree from Harvard University and a BA degree from UC Santa Cruz. He has studied seven languages. It's a life-long passion that began with a study of Spanish and continues with his ongoing studies of Chinese and Japanese.

Andrew has been involved in English education since 1993, both as a teacher and a writer. He has taught a variety of subjects, including English composition, business writing, English literature, and TOEFL preparation.

Andrew is the author of more than 30 English learning books, including classroom texts, supplementary books, self-study books, as well as TOEIC preparation texts. In addition to writing and teaching, he regularly attends ESL conferences and gives presentations to groups of teachers at schools and symposiums.

Central to Andrew's teaching philosophy is an emphasis on content. His work includes subjects from countries around the world, giving his writing an international flavor. Andrew also enjoys writing about cultural issues, as he is convinced of the vital link between language and culture.